Development Studies, Challenges and Education: An Integrated Approach

Mutubuki Edias Henry

Dedication

To the people of the world who strive to develop the citizens of the world and attempt to make the world one, as equals. May their efforts bear fruition and result in sustained socio economic progress for all.

Acknowledgements

It is proper that acknowledgement is made of persons who make commendable efforts in contributing to socio economic growth and development via different modes of project design, implementation and evaluation. They are so many in the world. But as charity begins at home, it is instructing to acknowledge the tremendous project works done by our own children as follows: Mukai Henrieta Mutubuki, currently the Senior Quantity Surveyor with one of the biggest construction companies in the United Arab Emirates; Chandi Mutubuki, Senior Project Manager with a leading Netherlands International Non Governmental Organization, working on green alternative, renewable energy projects in East and Southern Africa; Gamu Mutubuki, Senior Civil Engineer and designer of London road works; Fungai Mutubuki, Project Manager with a leading international property development company, specializing in accommodation solutions for domestic, commercial and industrial applications.

Development Studies, Challenges and Education: An Integrated Approach
Copyright © 2020 Mutubuki Edias Henry
Canadian Edition 2020
Published by Anetida Investments

ISBN: 978-1-7773403-2-2
Email Address: nematresort@gmail.com
Cover Design: Michael Kumirai

Foreword

Throughout my chequered life history and career, I have searched for a book that would cover personal, group, national and regional development issues. Here I have found a text that just does that. In this very important and timely book, the author engages topically, theoretically and practically extensive analytical perspectives on historical developments, current challenges, characteristics, intersections and possible solutions to Africa's socio economic crises. Cogently and brilliantly discussed in the book, the social, political and economic dimensions are intricately woven and interlinked with education. They inform and shape each other collectively helping or hindering socio economic growth and development. Hence, this august book provides scholarly information and insights for academics, practitioners, researchers; post graduate, graduate and undergraduate students.

It is indeed, with the complexity, which analytically juxtaposes the historical with the socio cultural, the political, the economic and the global issues, that one can ascertain the problems of development and education in contemporary Africa. The book is refreshingly candid, frank and akin to the Hard Talk series found in documentaries. Though the author acknowledges that some of the causes and effects of socio economic problems are externally driven, the weight of his criticism falls on internal governance issues, poor macro-economic policies, predatory corruption, and rent seeking activities by political and economic leadership. The author asserts that if Africa is to develop it needs to urgently shed off its nationalist autocratic dinosaurs with their myopic policies, and usher in youthful and progressive leadership.

The author paints a portrait of post colonial Africa that illustrates the mismatch between political policies, economic strategies and how the disconnect has devastating effects on social services, health and education. The arrival of new exploiters from China, Arab world and the Indian subcontinent has sharpened and deepened the plunder of Africa's resources.

The book endeavours to come up with practical strategies and workable solutions for reviving and stimulating socio economic growth and development in post colonial Africa in particular, and the under developed countries in general. This thoughtful and thought provoking treatise provides a very useful development road map for post colonial Africa and the developing world. Of particular interest to the reader are sections and advice on various forms and types of investment portfolios. These range from monetary, consumer, precious commodities to real asset investments.

When all is said and done, this is a fine book that is written by an astute and erudite scholar who is privy to many of the issues analyzed in this volume. The book responds powerfully and critically to many of the most important development issues facing post colonial Africa, and its populace. It fills a gaping space in contemporary development studies and education. As I have observed before, the book is exceptional in the way it highlights issues in education for development at the individual, group, national and regional levels.

Professor Ndawi, Obert, Paradzai
Zimbabwe Council for Higher Education.

Preface

There has perhaps never been a less propitious moment to present an introductory but comprehensive book on development studies, education and challenges than the present time. The world is awash with financial crises, conflict based socio economic cum political upheavals, poverty driven suffering and abject social inequalities. Increasingly, education is experiencing the intrusion of socio economic market philosophy. Hence, education is obliged to forge closer links with industry, commerce, and the world of work. So it is imperative that a student of social science acquire a working knowledge of the socio economic frameworks from which social, economic and educational challenges emerge.

The book is written from a firm conviction that economics and the world of business are of immense value to improving the lives of individuals, groups and nations. Towards these ends, the book provides a general background to the elements, theories and characteristics of socio economic growth and development. By surveying the social structures, their formations, their principal activities and problems, the book gives the student, and reader, a broad spectrum of the nature of the development world and the role of education in socio economic growth.

Further, the concern of the book is with attempting to answer the fundamental questions of what, why, who and how of socio economic growth, development and education. It is full of penetrating analyses of development issues at local, regional and international levels.

It is intended to be compulsory reading for students of socio economics, business management, entrepreneurship, development and education. Above all, it should be an essential tool, and constant companion, for those interested in investment issues and strategies. Armed with the knowledge, and skills, inherent in this book, the sky is the limit for those intending to get immersed in the field of socio economic growth and development. It acts as a spring board for budding entrepreneurs.

I have endeavoured to work on a natural free flow, and continuity in the development of topics. Included in the book are relevant topics on figures and statistics in socio economic growth, development and education. There is a relevant section on information, technology and communication as they relate to development studies. All these are relevant and topical to the student, and reader. Included at the end is a comprehensive, instructing and elaborate glossary of terms used, and implied, in the book. The glossary, in itself, is intended to act as a quick reference teaching and learning unit. The whole idea is to give a firm, substantive base for the student, and reader, as well as a balanced, integrated picture of development studies, socio economics, entrepreneurship and education.

Last but very important is the need to acknowledge the help, sources and encouragement from many people. No book is written in isolation, so I have benefited from contact, comments and discussions with a number of our students, colleagues and successful development practitioners. The temptation here would be to mention them by name, but the list would fill another volume. It suffices to say that I owe them my greatest debt. Nevertheless, at the end of the day, I bear the burden of any shortcomings, errors and omissions that remain.

Preface to the Canadian Edition

I wish to extend my profound gratitude to many readers' very useful suggestions. I have endeavoured to include the interesting, constructive and well meaning suggestions in the Canadian edition. It is also gratifying to note that the Canadian edition has come so soon. Canadian Edition is also available in e-book format.

I have made some additions and alterations to the first edition. By popular request I have added lengthy sections on agrarian reform, and Africa's contribution to civilization, education, economic growth and development. There are pressing needs for learning and understanding agrarian reform, country experiences, its effects on poverty, governance, economic growth and development.

Africa's contribution to civilization needs coverage of African contributions to metaphysical culture, material culture and literary thought. The world's three major monotheistic religions have been profoundly influenced by Egyptian Mephite theology. Egyptian literature immensely influenced European poetry, drama, story-telling and oral expositions. Also of great significance is Africa's immense contribution to physical and scientific culture as espoused in this august book.

A section on rules of thumb, relating to choice of socio economic projects, guides the reader to identify, choose and develop successful business projects. Today persons need to move away from life time employment and create socio economic projects that lead them to entrepreneurs. There is also an important addition that covers learning and teaching structures for outdoor world – an environmental friendly model to eco tourism ventures. The intention is to develop in people the need to value, appreciate, protect and conserve nature as a symbiotic enterprise that benefits everything and everyone in the cycle of the eco system. It is important that countryside people develop eco tourism ventures for general interest and income generation. Employment can be made in eco tourism ventures. Another useful addition is education for creating sustainable futures for all. Quality, inclusive, equitable education and lifelong learning are critical to sustainable socio economic, political and general development. Education is a key to the development process.

I have also provided more reading, tasks, and fresh emphases, seldom to introducing additions and alterations. I believe the book continues to challenge and stimulate the reader to wonder about social, economic, development and political issues you, the reader, might otherwise have ignored. As the wise African saying goes: There are three types of people in life; those who make things happen, those who watch things happen, and those who wonder what happened! This book tries to make the readers, make things happen.

E.H. Mutubuki.
Upon Nemat Holiday Resort: An ideal Pole of Growth.

Table of Contents

Understanding the Key Concepts

A book on development studies, challenges and education needs to explain the key concepts before delving into the intricacies of a subject that is so central to human endeavour.

Growth, development and education are vitally interlinked. Growth refers to personal, group and societal social, economic and psychological stages as one grows from infancy to adulthood in an attempt to be self sufficient. Growth can also refer to socio economic, political and infrastructural institutions as they move from one stage to the next. So growth involves activities, processes and products that may lead to development.

Development can be viewed as the process of improving the quality and quantity of peoples' lives and levels of social institutions. Hurlock (1997) says development refers to qualitative changes, which may be defined as a progressive series of orderly, coherent changes. Progressive implies that the changes are directional, and that they lead forward rather than backward. Orderly and coherent suggest that there is a definite relationship between the changes taking place and those that preceded or will follow them. So, effective development should lead to sustainable development, that is, development that meets the needs of the present without compromising the ability of future generations to meet their own needs. This should involve the infinite resource base feeding into the finite resource base. Infinite resources are of a permanent nature as opposed to finite resources that are expendable. Examples of infinite resources are wind, sunlight, water, people; and finite resources minerals, fauna, flora, cash.

Stages of Growth and Development

There are three basic stages of growth and development. Stage one involves attempts to meet the basic needs, such as, food, safe water, shelter, sanitation, basic health and education. Stage two concerns itself with basic infrastructure like roads, bridges, power, transport system and communication. Stage three involves scientific and technological advancement like inventions, discoveries and creativity. In highly developed countries there is the emergence of stage four involving surpluses and excesses in products of growth, such as, food, litter, obesity, idleness, pollution, entertainment and aging population. This stage is a sign of over development. On the other hand, when a people, or a country, fail to meet the first three stages they are considered to be under developed. (McClelland, 1989).

Sustainable Development and Education

For there to be sustainable development that has momentum, education is vital. Sustainable development process is propelled and maintained by education. The term education comes from Latin word *educare*, which means to nurture, to look after wholly and carefully. So, society nurtures the people and their institutions using education in all its forms, that is, formal, informal and non formal. In other words, education can be viewed as the vehicle that conveys the norms, values, ethos, knowledge and skills that are needed for development, of the individual and people in society. Hence, being educated implies civilized behaviour, academic and professional accomplishment, possession of a sound, reliable and upright character, maturity and responsibility. One should also be well versed in the traditions and ways of life of the people, be tolerant and accommodating, be open to other points of view; should spend time and resources profitably and wisely.

For further expansion on key concepts refer to glossary section.

As we have seen above, development is about the quality and quantity of life, life span, life expectancy, survival of the individual and the species, and the human race. There is also the need to understand the symbiotic nature of life, the place of people, fauna, flora and the elements in the scheme of life and things. Development should be viewed in the context of the eco system that deals with the inter connections and interrelationships of living organisms and their environment. There is the close connection existing between all that happens on the planet earth as a result of human action or goodwill, or lack of it. Biodiversity teaches us to appreciate and respect the variety, and symbiotic nature, of life forms that exist within the eco system.

It is instructing to briefly trace human history and its effects on planet earth and the biosphere. Evolving from a pre-human ancestor that lived about two million years ago in the tropics of Africa, the human race spread out over the whole face of the earth. But most of this spread has taken place only in the last ten thousand years. Modern person, *homo sapiens sapiens*, evolved into five races, namely, the Congoids, Mongoloids, Caucasoids, Capoids and Australoids. They spread from Africa, Asia and into Europe, America and Australasia. Taking advantage of the shifting ice age and moving game they spread all over the globe.

The modern person's mastery of the technologies of fire, shelter, clothing, tools and artefacts has led to civilizations, manufacturing and love of creature comfort. However, the wanton increase in manufacturing, mining, agriculture, and technologies has led to ecological harm, some of it, irreversible. Examples are pollution, nuclear fall out, the destruction of the ozone layer, the fast melting ice in the Arctic and Antarctic regions, rising water levels and floods threatening many islands, and coastal lands with submergence.

So, development studies is about knowing causes and effects of human action, or lack of it, of differentials in income, and expenditure, of disparities in living standards between peoples of the world. There is also the pressing need to learn about, and understand the social, economic, political and ideological dynamics of the world we live, and die, in. A student of development studies has to understand the context of conflict, the causes, effects and how to mitigate them. There is also the need to map out strategies to avoid dehumanizing experiences of war, migration, human trafficking, dependency, poverty, debt, donor syndrome, and hunger.

Yet another good reason for engaging in development studies is that we learn a lot from others. Development specialists, theorists, strategists and their case studies teach us a lot. As Isaac Newton said, 'If I have been able to see, to perceive further than others, it is because I have stood on the shoulders of intellectual giants!'

For discussion

Discuss three reasons that make you want to study economic, development and education issues.

Development Indicators and Patterns

Development is more than simply increasing economic out put. It is a wider concept than economic growth. Even if a country's economy experiences growth of Gross Domestic Product it does not mean that economic development is taking place. So, wider and more composite indicators of development need correlating with other crucial indicators like GDP per capita.

Single Indicators of Development

There are a number of single indicators that can be used to measure the extent to which people of a country are experiencing challenges of development. These focus on one area of socio economic development. For example, focus can be put on Gross Domestic Product, which is a measure of economic activity, and of national income. It is the total value of all goods and services produced over a given period, usually a year, excluding net property income from outside the country. It can be measured either as the total of income, expenditure or output.

Gross National Product is a measure of economic activity and national income. GNP is the total value of all goods and services produced over a given time period, usually a year, including net property income from outside the country. It can be measured either as the total of income, expenditure or output.

Balance of payments is a record of income and expenditure transactions between people outside a country and those inside a country. The balance of payments accounts record all flows of money in and out of a country. These flows might result from the sale of exports, called an inflow or credit, or from a country's purchasing imports from outside a country, called an outflow or debit. The flows may also arise from other countries investing in a country, called inward investment credit. It may also be from a country's companies investing outside, called outward investment debit. It should be noted that all flows of money are added and grouped according to their type. The over all account is then called the balance of payments. This is because the total of outflows should be equivalent to the total of inflows. The balance of payments, therefore balances. When the outflows are more than the inflows it is a sign and indicator of a country's economic problems. In other words, the balance of trade, which is the difference between the value of visible exports and visible imports, is in trouble.

Budget deficit is a situation where government expenditure exceeds government income. Government income comes from taxation and other revenues. Hence, its sources are finite. Most of the time budget deficits are a result of unbridled expenditure on defence, education, health, social welfare, and financial indiscipline.

Capital account is that part of the balance of payments accounts that measures the flows of capital in and out of a country. Capital constitutes human made resources like money, machinery, factories, and offices. So, capital is one of the vital factors of production. Capital flight is the movement of financial assets out of a country in response to perceived unfavourable domestic policies and circumstances. Investors are highly sensitive to what they perceive to be a threat to investment and profit. Many development problems, of less developed countries, lie in poor macro-economic policies. Policies emanating from government laws, pronouncements and manifestos, such as indigenisation of land, agriculture, mining, industry and commerce can be detrimental to development. Development and wealth cannot be given to people on a platter. It should be earned through enterprise, hard work, skills in wealth creating, work ethics and morality. All this should improve the circular flow of income and expenditure in a country.

Circular flow of income is the flow of income and payments between economic agents in an economy. The key agents are households and firms, and the circular flow shows how money moves between them. There may be leakages from the circular flow, and injections into it. Leakages are income not passed on by consumers in the circular flow. Examples are savings, taxation, money spent on imports. Leakages can also be called withdrawals from the circular flow. Injections are an addition to the income of firms which does not normally arise from the expenditure of households. Examples are changes in investment, state spending, or exports. A healthy economy should show strong and consistent circular flow of income. Consumption should show consistent flows. Consumption is expenditure by households on goods and services which satisfy current wants. It is a key component of aggregate demand. Aggregate demand is the total of all planned expenditure in an economy at each level of prices. It is the total level of demand in the economy. The main groups in the economy who spent are consumers, firms which spend on investment, government expenditure, and people who export.

Demand is the want or need for a product that is backed by an ability to pay. Demand is measured over a given time period. It is determined by a number of factors such as income, tastes, choice, and the price of substitute and complementary goods available. However, certain goods are demerit goods in that authorities consider them harmful to consumers; products such as drugs and alcohol which consumers may over value but have detrimental effects. On the other hand merit goods such as education, health and sanitation may not attract demand as much as consumer goods. Consumers may under value them, while authorities believe them to be essential for individual and national development. But, merit goods tend to be under valued by market forces and the public in general.

Aggregate demand is the total of all planned expenditure in an economy at each level of prices. So it is the total level of demand in the economy. In other words it is the total of all desired expenditure at any time by all groups in the economy. The main groups that spend are domestic consumers, firms, government, exporters. On the other hand, aggregate supply is the total quantity supplied at every price level. It is the total of all goods and services produced in an economy in a given period.

Linked to all this is income elasticity of demand. This measures the responsiveness of demand to a given change in income. It is an important piece of information to a firm as it helps them to predict how much the demand for their product will grow as the economy grows. Income elasticity is calculated thus: Income elasticity of demand = % change in demand / % change in the level of income. If the figure is greater than 1 then the product is described as income elastic or income sensitive. This means that demand will grow by more than the level of income. If on the other hand, the figure is less than 1 then the product is described as income inelastic. So, the demand will grow less than the level of income. Another related indicator is price elasticity of demand. This measures the responsiveness of demand to a given change in price. It is calculated by taking the percentage change in demand and dividing by the percentage change in price.

Linked to fluctuations in supply and demand is inflation. Inflation is the general rise in prices and the reduction in value of money. Inflation is a sustained increase in the general price level. In other words it is the rate at which prices are increasing. Inflation can be measured monthly, quarterly, or yearly. It is usually measured by a price consumer index through a basket of basic consumer items. There are two forms of inflation. Demand pull inflation occurs when aggregate demand exceeds aggregate supply. If there is an excess demand in the economy, this tends to cause prices to rise. Thus demand pull inflation is essentially a case of too much money chasing too few goods. The second form of inflation is called cost push inflation where a cost of production increases and the seller has to put up prices to maximise profits. Cost of production factors are wages, raw materials, energy, and fuel. Cost push inflation can occur independent of demand. Deflation is the opposite of inflation in that there is a sustained general fall in prices and increase in value of money. This tends to lead to increased savings leading to investment, thus stimulating the economy.

Cost benefit analysis is a method of assessing investment projects which takes into account social costs and benefits. Investment is the purchase of capital resources such as land, factories, mines, equipment, machinery that firms need to produce. Investment is usually split into two parts: Replacement investment deals with replacing machinery, equipment, furnaces and so on; net investment is where investors start new, and innovative, enterprises. Net investment adds directly to the capital stock of the economy. To ailing economies net investment is direct inoculation. It should start up and invigorate ailing and moribund economies. Investment can also refer to changes in the level of stocks.

Crude birth rate (CBR) is the number of children born alive each year per 1000 of the population. Another term linked to this one is called fertility rate. This is the number of children born alive per 1000 women per year. Crude death rate (CDR) is the yearly number of deaths per 1000 of the population. Infant mortality rates measure the rate at which children being born in a country are dying. Infant mortality is often used as a measure of how well developed the health system of a country is. A low CBR is a good measure of the quality of life a country enjoys, and a high CDR is an indicator of lack of quality of life.

Dependency ratio is the ratio of dependent population, such as the young, infirm and elderly, to the working age population. This can be an indicator of development challenges. Life expectancy is the average length of time that people in a country are expected to live, barring an accident. The average life expectancy for a person in a highly developed country is 75 years whereas that of a person in a poor country would be 34. This shows clearly disparities in the quality of life between nations.

Exchange rate is the price of one currency in terms of another. For example the exchange rate between the British pound and the US dollar may be 1 to 1.60. The term exchange rate can also be used to refer to the price at which any good is traded for another good. Exchange rates can be fixed or floating. The term fixed, means that the exchange rates stay at the same value as set by the state. This is artificial and creates problems for the economy. This is exchange control in that the state controls the amount of foreign currency available to local firms or citizens.

The term floating, means that the exchange rates fluctuate on a day to day basis according to the market. Dual exchange rate is a system where there is a fixed official exchange rate and an illegal market determined parallel exchange rate. This is common in command economies where the state owns and controls resources. This system leads to problems of development such as inefficiency, corruption, misallocation of resources, speculative behaviour and greed. All this affects factors of production greatly.

Factors of production are the resources that are necessary for production. They are normally classified into 4 groups: Land and all natural resources like minerals, raw materials, water; capital includes human made resources such as money, machinery, buildings, factories, equipment and expertise; labour include knowledge, skills, work ethics; enterprise includes entrepreneurial ability, postponement of gratification. It is very important to note that the rate of economic growth and development are affected by the quantity and quality of the factors of production. This refers to productivity.

Productivity is a crucial aspect of economic growth and development. Productivity is the efficiency with which the factors of production are used. It can be calculated by taking total output and dividing by the number of factors of production. The higher the figure, the more productive the factors of production are. This has trickle down effects that stimulate the country's economy. Trickle down effect is the process whereby the economic gains from economic growth pass down through out the entire society eventually giving rise to development.

Composite Indicators of Living Standards and Development

We discussed a number of single indicators above. These tend to focus on one area at a time such as economy, education, health and environment. This approach, though useful for academic purposes, seems cumbersome and repetitive. Individual indicators invariably fail to consider all the necessary characteristics of challenges to economic growth and development. So, development experts have consequently attempted to construct measures, or indices, that combine many of the individual indicators. These are called composite indicators. So a number of composite indices have been developed that allow several indicators and measures to be aggregated. This gives a more comprehensive measure of living standards and quality of life. This is the primary concern of all developers.

The Physical Quality of Life Index (PQLI)

In this index three single indicators are combined, that is, life expectancy at birth, infant mortality and literacy rates. It is a composite indicator of development. For each indicator the performance of individual countries are rated on a scale of 1 to 100, where 1 represents the worst and 100 the best. Though it has correlations with GDP per capita, it is not as accurate as expected.

The Human Development Index (HDI)

This is a human development index based on real GDP per capita, life expectancy at birth and educational achievement that measure socio economic development. The index, produced by the United Nations Development Programme, also includes indicators of longevity, knowledge and income. Some countries have shown rapid economic growth but fail to measure up to the requirements of HD index. Countries are rated on a scale of 0 to 1, where 0 represents the worst and 1 the best. A comparison of a few countries shows wide disparities in development.

Country	Year	Human Development Index	Real GDP per capita (US $)
Japan	2010	0.920	25000
Switzerland	2010	0.910	26400
United States	2010	0.860	21500
Zimbabwe	2010	0.544	500
India	2010	0.550	640

UNDP 2010

The Human Suffering Index (HSI)

This index is used by organisation like the World Health Organization, Care International and the UN Human Habitat. The index ranks people according to the level of human suffering based on 10 measures: life expectancy, daily calorie supply, access to clean water, primary school enrolment, per capita GDP, rate of inflation, communications, technology, Civil rights and rule of law, political freedom. Most poor countries score very low whilst advanced countries score very high. Africa, in particular, suffers from governance issues, repression, lack of freedom, corruption, intolerance, crime and violence. All these hinder human and economic development.

Human Poverty Index (HPI)

This is a composite index that measures human deprivation. The United Nations defines poverty as the denial of choices and opportunities most basic to human development to lead a long healthy, creative life and enjoy a decent standard of living, freedom, self esteem and the respect of others. The Human Poverty index is aimed at seeing the level of deprivation and poverty being experienced in a country. There are two HPI indices that are used.

HPI -1 is a measure of absolute poverty used in less developed countries. Absolute poverty is a level of poverty when only the minimum levels of food, clothing and shelter can barely be met. The variables used are: The percentage of people expected to die before the age of 40; the percentage of people who are illiterate; deprivation in over all socio economic provisioning in private and public institutions. These should be reflected by the percentage of people without access to health services, sanitation, safe water, and the number of under nourished children.

HPI -2 is a measure of relative poverty used in more advanced countries. Relative poverty is the level of poverty in a country expressed in terms of certain levels of income. It focuses on relative deprivation in the same three dimensions as HPI -1 with an adjusted set of criteria. HPI -2 has a fourth variable, social exclusion measured by low incomes and long durations of unemployment. The variables for HPI -2 are: the percentage of people likely to die before age 60; the percentage of people who cannot effectively read and write; the proportion of people with disposable incomes of less than 50% of the median population; and the proportion of long term unemployment, that is, 12 months or more.

Alternative Indicators of Poverty

There are other ways of measuring levels of poverty and development in the world. The indicators fall into two categories. The first category is on health and education indicators. The second measures access to, and impact of education on individuals.

1. Measures of Good Health

These include infant mortality rates that measure the number of live born babies who do not survive to their first birthday out of 1000 babies born in total. This measure is linked to life expectancy, at birth, rated as the average number of years a new born baby can expect to live if conditions remain the same. The main cause of malnutrition and poor health is the lack of quality and variety of calories and proteins taken a day. Many countries, especially in Africa, and the Indian sub continent, suffer from malnutrition, hunger and even starvation. The general populace lack foods with enough calorific and nutritional value. Lack of a balanced diet, especially in children, can lead to poor mental and intellectual development.

Access to quality medical care, such as hospitals, clinics and doctors are critical to human health and life expectancy. The indicators cover the number of doctors, and hospital beds, per 100 000 of the population available to citizens of a country under consideration.

2. Measures of access to, and impact of education

Here education is viewed as the main vehicle of socio economic growth and development. So, literacy rates are central to measures of access to, and impact of education. The percentage of the population over the age of 15 who can read, calculate and write is measured in terms of primary school enrolment, retention and completion. Primary, adult and basic education is viewed by the United Nations as a basic human right. So the general populace is expected to be able to read, write and calculate if a country is to develop.

Question for Reflection

What would you consider to be most relevant indicators for you and your country?

Country Classification and Main Characteristics

There are wide disparities in the growth rates of nations resulting in sizeable income and development gaps. The causes of these wide disparities would range from historical, governance, social, cultural, economic, to political reasons. So the causes could be externally based and internally imposed. Some less developed countries have been able to improve their economic conditions over time and become more developed. On the other hand some more developed countries have experienced a sharp decline in economic growth and standard of living, mainly due to self inflicted policies. Socio political driven policies have driven the countries aground resulting in poverty, neglect and misery. This leads to instability and mayhem. The most dramatic falls in socio economic and standards of living can be seen in post independent countries, especially in Africa, which have pursued passion-led policies instead of prudent driven ones.

The most dramatic rises in economic growth and standards of living are seen in countries that have exercised prudent socio economic policies and programmes. Post Second World War Japan and West Germany rose from ashes to riches in a space of 50 years. The 'little dragons' of Asia, Taiwan, South Korea, Hong Kong and Singapore have shown what can be done through correct choice of production cum market driven programmes. They now constitute the Newly Industrialized nations of the world after adopting the Japanese model of development. The lessons to be drawn from the above success stories is that any country in the world can lift itself by the boot straps, even by the toes, to great socio economic heights through shear hard work, prudent and wise policies and programmes.

It is true that most developing countries face daunting obstacles as they try to compete in the global economy. World macro economics bring with them disparities in income, technology, expertise and financial fundamentals. But all countries of the world had to experience similar obstacles at some stage of development.

Country Classification

There is considerable socio economic inequality among countries in the world. The richest 20% of the world's population receive about 80% of the world's resources and income. There are many different ways of classifying countries of the world. Here we can use the World Bank's country classification which puts countries into four groups.

Group 1 constitutes industrially advanced countries (IACs) characterized by well developed market driven economies based on large stocks of capital goods, advanced technology for production and well educated workers. These high income countries are Japan, Germany, United States of America, Canada, United Kingdom, Russia, Australia and most countries of Western Europe.

Their Per Capita Income averages $26 000, literacy rates are more than 90%, and life expectancy is 75% and more. Malnutrition rates are 1%, with most of the population enjoying high standards of living such as good sanitation, safe running water, good shelter, sound education, high standards of health service and leisure activities.

Group 2 belong to Oil Exporting Countries (OECs) which are not highly industrialised but have high per capita incomes (GDP). Examples of these OECs are Saudi Arabia, United Arab Emirates, Kuwait, Iraq, Iran, and Venezuela. They enjoy a high standard of living because of income from exporting oil to the world, mainly IACs who use the oil for vehicles, ships, machinery, equipment, and heating purposes. They used to have a powerful grouping called Organization of Petroleum Exporting Countries (OPEC) that would determine prices per barrel of oil, production levels, policy leverage. But their power and influence have declined because of a number of factors like more oil producers have come on the scene, instability in the Arab world, fast discoveries of alternative energy sources such as shale gas for engines, solar, hydro and wind energy. The OECs have also to re-strategise and diversify their economies given the fact that fossil fuels eventually run out of supply and fashion. If they do not they run the risk of regressing to under development levels.

Group 3 has come into play by taking on board the Japanese model of development that concentrates on adding value to imported products like iron, chrome, aluminium and steel. With these imports they make durable vehicles, ships, machinery, technological equipment for self and export. These Newly Industrialised countries (NICs) sometimes referred to as the 'Little Dragons of Asia' are Taiwan, Singapore, Hong Kong, South Korea. They have tremendously improved the quality and quantity of the lives of their people. They provide excellent lessons for the developing nations, especially in Africa, that export raw materials to these countries, America and Europe, instead of adding value to the vast resources they have.

Group 4 constitutes the largest number of countries in the world. They number over 100 countries and constitute 75% of the world's population. They are found in Africa, Asia, Central and South America, the Pacific and Atlantic islands. They are kindly referred to as Developing Countries (DCs) and frankly called Less Developed Countries (LDCs). The difference between the DCs nd LDCs is the same. They share common characteristics and development indicators. They have low literacy rates, high mortality rates, high unemployment rates, low labour productivity, rapid population growth, poor health and nutrition, poor sanitation and water reticulation, low life expectancy. Their exports consist of raw materials and unfinished products. They use backward technology and machinery as they produce mainly to subsist. They are characterised by lack of sophistication, unequal distribution of incomes, corruption, greed and lawlessness leading to socio political instability. All these lead to vicious cycles of poverty, human suffering and under development.

The happiest countries in the world

The United Nations Sustainable Development Solutions Network started reporting annual happiness reviews in 2012. The reports have received acclamation by human rights groups, development agencies and socio economists the world over. It is also referred to as the world Smile report. The report uses six measurements to calculate people happiness. The measures are: Healthy life expectancy, social support, absence of corruption, freedom to make life choices, generosity, GDP per capita.

The 2017 UN world happiest countries report listed 20 happiest countries:

1. Norway;
2. Denmark (has won top position 4 times before);
3. Iceland;
4. Switzerland;
5. Finland;
6. Netherlands;
7. Canada
8. New Zealand
9. Australia;
10. Sweden;
11. Israel (will fall way down with Palestinian racist, uncontrolled land annexation) 12. Costa Rica;
13. Austria;
14. USA (May fall very low because of Donald Trump Amerex from global outings, racist, religious policies);
15. Ireland;
16. Germany (with its rich technology, the Rhine Valley and Angela Merkel open door humanitarian policies);
17. Belgium;
18. Luxembourg;
19. United Kingdom (will drop dramatically with its Brexit from the European Union, tough immigration policies. May lose UK status with Scotland and Ireland breaking away to remain in the EU);
20. Chile.

It is not a happy event to comment on the unhappiest countries of the world. The sad, weeping nations would be in the Middle East, Far East like North Korea, China, Russia under Vladmir Putin, many countries in South America and Africa.

For reflection

What lessons do less developed nations learn from the experiences of Newly Industrialised Nations? Suggest, and justify ways in which Africa should remove sad and weeping cases of its people.

Development Theory

Development theory evolved from the need and desire to explain economic, production and social factors that promote or hinder human endeavours in development. Humanity has always been interested in wealth creation and improvement of people's lives. Ancient civilizations like Egypt, Sumeria, Incas, Greece, Rome and Zimbabwe were preoccupied with socio economic growth and development. Their rise, and eventual fall, were in the main, linked to socio economic growth and development. Adam Smith in 1776 asked the pertinent question: What determined the wealth of people and nations? Alfred Marshall in 1890 got involved in the quest for growth as it gave economic studies their chief, and highest, interests. Robert Lucas, as late as 1989, has said that once one starts to think about economic growth and development, it is hard to think about anything else.

After the Second World War, with many developing countries becoming independent, policy experts, having ignored poor countries for centuries, called for urgent attention to growth and development problems. Two historical events greatly influenced the first generation development economists. First, the Great Depression led to sharp rises in unemployment, poverty and suffering. Second, the fast rise of the Soviet Union, through forced saving and investment evoked fear of the spread of communism to other countries. Of particular concern to the West was the potential appeal of communist and socialist ideologies to developing countries, especially newly independent ones. The Soviet growth model seemed to be working well. So the quest for growth and development theory from the Western point of view became imperative.

The above notwithstanding, theories help us to unravel the complexities of economic development. Theories act as mirrors through which we examine ourselves and others in an effort to mend our ways, correct our course of action and redirect our efforts towards effective management of human and natural resources. They make us reflect on failures and successes in human socio economic enterprises.

So a development theory is a set of reasoned ideas intended to explain social facts, economic events, production processes leading to success or failure of a system or institution. In this chapter we look at a development theorist's ideas, reflect on them, give a critique of the strengths and limitations so as to arrive at a reasonable conclusion. The main idea is to glean the grain from the chaff and be able to plant the seed of growth and development for our benefit.

Malthus Thomas and the Model of Demographic Transition

Thomas Robert Malthus (1766-1834) was a British scholar who had tremendous influence in socio political economy. He attended Jesus College, Cambridge, and came out with distinctions in Mathematics and Classics. He later on was ordained an Anglican priest. His theory of unchecked population growth leading to a forced return to below subsistence level conditions influenced Charles Darwin's biological theory of evolution and survival of the fittest.

In 1798 the Reverend Thomas Robert Malthus described the stages in the relationship between birth and death rates and the over all population change. The growth in the population due to changes in the birth and death rates is called the natural rate of population growth. The model for demographic transition suggested that a population's mortality and fertility would decline as a result of social and economic development. Malthus examined the effects of population growth and reached a sombre conclusion that population growth would naturally check itself in the form of famine, wars and disease.

His main premise was that populations tended to grow by geometric progression, that is, 2, 4, 8, 16, 32, 64. Whilst resources like land to produce food tended to increase by arithmetic progression, then stop, that is, 2, 4, 6, 8, 10. So through time and natural selection populations would outstrip food resources leading to the law of diminishing returns. His law of diminishing returns stated that increasing amounts of a factor input such as fertilizer or labour to a fixed factor as land, the marginal product of the input would eventually diminish. In other words, the increase in the output of land, the crop yields, would progressively decrease. That is why Malthus' theory is sometimes referred to as the theory of diminishing returns.

Malthus also predicted that all countries of the world would over time go through four demographic transition stages. Stage 1, is pre-industrialisation marked by unstable population growth, with high birth rates because there is no family planning. Parents have many children because few survive. Other reasons are that many children, and wives, are needed to work the land. Children are also viewed as a sign of virility and wealth. Some religious and cultural traditions encourage large families. But this stage is also marked by high death rates due to disease and plagues because of poor hygiene, lack of safe drinking water and sewage disposal. Other causes are famine, malnutrition, poor diet, and uncertain food supplies.

Stage 2, is rapid population growth because of high birth rates. The reasons are the same as in stage 1. But there are falling death rates because of improved medical care such as vaccinations, hospitals, medicines, doctors. There is improved sanitation, safe water supplies and accommodation. There are improvements in food production in terms of quantity and quality. All these factors would lead to marked decrease in child mortality rates.

Stage 3, is decreasing population growth due to falling birth rates because of wide spread use of family planning practices such as contraceptives, sterilisation, legalised abortions and other incentives. Emancipation of women leads to control of number of children. Lower infant mortality rates mean less pressure to have many children. Death rates are low across the board.

Stage 4, is industrialisation marked by stable, low population growth due to low birth rates. The reasons are the same as in stage 3. In this stage there is increased mechanisation and industrialisation with less need for manual and menial labour. There is also increased desire for material possessions, creature comfort and less desire for large families. Death rates are very low across the board.

Using Malthus' theory we see that LDCs have moved through stage 1 and are at stage 2. Most are struggling to move to stage 3. Many LDC countries maintain high birth rates to make up for rising death rates due to endemics like HIV/Aids, and worsening poverty, wars, hunger.

Multhus' theory has a lot of relevance to present day world development problems. Demographic pressures bring in aging populations in developed countries as a result of successful family planning, whereas young bulging populations of less developed countries put a lot of pressures on resources. As a consequence migration pressures from less developed countries to developed countries alleviate many of the social problems of host countries. However, these migration pressures do trigger nationalism, xenophobia and resentment in host countries.

Limitations of Malthus' theory

The main criticism of Malthus' theory is that it fails to take into account other equally important pressures on national, regional and global development. Examples are environmental degradation, food shortages, and socio economic inequalities. Environmental pressures on planet earth result in pollution, degradation, rising water levels, destruction of the ozone layer, reduction in land for agriculture, changes in weather patterns, scarcity of water, all inhibit development. Food pressures emanate from the above mentioned pressures, to combine with poor governance and misplaced macro economic policies leading to food production reduction. Socio economic inequalities between rich world and poor world, disparities in income within nations, unemployment, differential educational and health provision lead to social springs. In short Malthus' theory is lopsided in that it leaves out other factors of development by concentrating on demography.

The other limitation is that the stages are linear suggesting that once a stage is passed there is no going back. As a matter of observation countries that have reached stages 3 or 4 have regressed to stage 2. Reasons for regression could be conflict, wars, natural calamities, or sheer mismanagement and irresponsible behaviour by those in authority.

The other short-comings of Malthus' analysis are that he assumed static technology and innovation. Improved technologies, fertilisers, pesticides, sophisticated machinery and horticultural techniques have made production demand and supply go beyond increases in population.

Another criticism of the Malthusian theory centres on terms that carry a pejorative connotation indicating excessive pessimism bordering on inhumanity. Marxists argue that Malthus seemed to argue for self centred grab of resources by the strongest elements of society, with no remorse or conscience.

Rostow Walt's Model- the Stages of Economic Development

In 1960, the American economic historian, W.W. Rostow suggested that countries passed through five stages of economic development. Rostow emphasised that development requires substantial investment in capital. He painted a portrait of what an economy should be through the five stages. It was an expansion of Malthus' stages of demographic transition.

Stage 1 Traditional Society where the economy is dominated by subsistence activity. The bulk of the output is consumed by producers rather than traded. Trade is carried out by barter where goods are exchanged directly for other goods. In this set up agriculture is the predominant activity. Hence, production is labour intensive utilising limited quantities of capital. Resource allocation, such as land and water, is determined by traditional methods of production.

Stage 2, the Preconditions for Take-off (Transitional Stage) where there is increased specialisation begins to generate surpluses for trading. There is an emergence of communications and transport infrastructure to service the growing trade. As incomes, savings and investment grow entrepreneurs emerge. But trade occurs concentrating on primary products and raw materials.

Stage 3, Take Off where industrialisation increases with workers moving from agriculture to the manufacturing and commercial sectors. Growth of industry, commerce and social institutions is concentrated in a few regions of the country. The levels of incomes, savings and investment reach over 10% of GDP. The growth is self sustaining as investment leads to increasing incomes generating more savings to finance further investment. The economic transitions are accompanied by the evolution of new political and social institutions that support the industrialisation and commercialisation. The emergence of interest groups like workers and employers' movements take centre stage. Legal and judicial systems to arbitrate and adjudicate contested issues emerge.

Stage 4, Drive to Maturity is the stage where the economy is diversifying into new areas. Technological innovation provides a diverse range of windows and opportunities for investment. The economy is now producing a wide range of goods and services. Educational institutions range from primary, secondary and tertiary levels to serve the needs and interests of commerce and industry. Curricula changes are tailored to suit the new socio economic order. The country's balance of payments are now highly favourable since the country exports more than it imports. A level of self sufficiency is reached where there are surpluses of food leading to new forms of health problems.

Stage 5, High Mass Consumption, the economy is fully geared towards mass consumption. Mass goods, foods and consumables dominate the market. This leads to waste and pollution. Waste management systems emerge to deal with increases in waste like plastics, broken glass, chemicals and machine parts, industrial pollution. Food production and outlets churn out junk food harmful to consumers. Health problems like obesity, coronary diseases, hypertension, diabetes rise. Health services emerge to deal with these new problems, raking in substantial amounts of cash. Because of high efficiency in industrial and commercial production leisure time has to be managed. Hence, the emergence of an entertainment industry in music, film, dance, sport and games. Investments in sporting arena, music centres, entertainment shows, film and acting arts proliferate.

A Critique of Rostow's Theory

Rostow's theory puts a finger on critical issues which are relevant to development. It succeeds in pin pointing areas needing developing. However, Rostow's theory views development as linear and cast in strait jacket. Once a country has reached a stage it remains there. But experience has shown that development is cyclical with some countries leap-froging the stages to reach greater heights of economic development. Examples are post World War Two Japan and Germany, the Little Dragons of Asia. Conversely countries can regress to lower stages of economic development. Examples are post colonial countries in Sub Saharan Africa that have sunk to lower levels than at independence. Many development economists argue that Rostow's model assumed high levels of sophistication. It was developed with western socio cultures in mind. It lacks details on the nature of the pre-conditions for growth. It is not strong as a predictive model of growth and development.

Nevertheless, it is useful as it highlights the need for steady and regular shots of investment. It should also be noted that, like many models of economic development, it is essentially a growth model which does not address the issues of development in general, nor specific contexts. It does not take into account social and group dynamics prevalent in developing countries.

Fisher and Clark's Theory of Structural Change

Two economists, Fisher, A. G.B. (1933) and Clark, C. (1940) developed the same theory over a period of time.

The Fisher-Clark Hypothesis

Fisher and Clark stated that workers in pre-industrial societies were predominantly involved in the primary sector, particularly agriculture. As industrialization occurs in a society employment becomes concentrated in the manufacturing, or secondary sector. In a post industrial society manufacturing becomes less important. The service, or tertiary, sector gains prominence. The three sector hypothesis of socio economics was based largely on the model. The model provides a description of the types of activities important in all societies. The model also describes how the economy changes over time, and how this changes the activities of the society.

The theory is based on changes in the structure of a country. The structure is viewed in three dimensions, one feeding into the other. The first is physical structure composed of infrastructure such as buildings, roads, rail, seaports, airports, bridges, dams and reservoirs. Their presence, or absence, is checked for advancement, efficiency and sophistication. The second is the social structure which is composed of education, commerce, industry, personnel skills and levels of income, health services, water and sewer reticulation. The third is the other structures which include power, grids, power plants like hydro, thermal and nuclear stations, water purification, sewer treatment and disposal plants.

Structural change of an economy here refers to a long term, macro level shift in the fundamental structure of an economic system. For example, a subsistence economy is transformed into a manufacturing economy; or a regulated mixed economy is liberalised. A current structural change in the world economy is globalisation.

Fisher and Clark put forward the idea that an economy of a country would have three stages of production. The first is primary production which is concerned with the extraction of raw materials through agriculture, mining, fishing and forestry. Primary refers to harvesting, or gathering of natural resources. So the primary sector involves the use of physical space, or the withdrawal of materials from the physical space. Low income countries are predominantly dominated by primary production. Countries are assumed to first pass through the primary production stage.

Then they move to the secondary production stage that is concerned with industrial production through manufacturing and construction. In this stage of production, natural resources are processed, or refined for further use. Assembly, construction and baking for example, are part of the secondary sector, which uses products from the primary sector to create consumer goods. Middle income countries are often dominated by the secondary sector. As economies develop and incomes rise then the demand for agricultural goods will increase. But due to the low incomes, elasticity of demand falls to just consumption levels. However, demand for manufactured goods will have a proportionately higher income elasticity of demand. So as incomes grow the demand for these goods will eventually grow at a higher rate. Hence, the secondary industry will grow leading to the third stage of production.

The tertiary production stage is concerned with the provision of services such as education, commerce, retail, banking, and tourism. So the tertiary sector involves services related to the other two sectors. This sector does not involve production, but rather provides support for that occurs in the first and second sectors. In high income countries the tertiary sector dominates. So having a large tertiary sector is viewed as a sign of economic maturity in the development process. As incomes continue to grow with prosperity all round, people will start to consume and have more services as these have an even higher income elasticity of demand. Hence, the tertiary sector will grow and develop. Here ends the Fisher Clark model of development as it stood.

The quaternary and quinary sectors

Later, theorists P. Hatt and N.Foote added the quaternary and quinary sectors to the Fisher-Clark economic model. The two theorists felt that the tertiary, or service, sector was overly large, and should be divided up. The quaternary sector refers to intellectuals, or information related positions. So its services include health care, education, government, and information technology. The quinary sector refers to top level executives in any part of the service sector, including chief executive officers, managing directors, presidents, cabinet ministers, high level government officials, education, and health care administrators.

However, this may be misleading. Some Less Developed countries may have a large tertiary, quaternary and quinary sectors due to high income from oil, or mining or tourism industry without having developed a secondary industry. Such fragile economies have inherent risks. If an economic base is dominated by an activity that has a high income elasticity of demand, an economic down turn such as recession in the consuming nations will have serious effects on the country's export earnings. If such country does not have secondary industry to fall back on, the reduction in demand for the tertiary services will have severe effects on the economy. (Pasinetti, 1981).

Limitations of the Theory

The theory assumes that development is linear. In reality development can be cyclical as it can either progress or regress. It does not take into account that individuals, and firms, in some countries hedge against risky eventualities through diversification of production and varied investment portfolios.

The theory also assumes that persons in all countries have the same levels of sophistication in terms of levels of commitment, motivation, self starting strategies and self correcting mechanisms. A number of people think they have reached the apex of Maslow's hierarchy of needs when they attain some goals in life. To them self actualisation is the end. But real success is when one has gone beyond self actualisation to reach an even higher stage called self transcending. To transcend is to go beyond self, what benefits the individual, and leave a legacy. People like that are found in countries that develop the skills and entrepreneurship to reach self transcending. For innovation is 20% ideas and 80% enterprise and execution.

The model has shown that too much concentration on, and of, the tertiary, quaternary and quinary sectors can be counter productive. Countries that have recently suffered socio economic down turns, recessions and depression have had over reliance on the tertiary sector, and particularly the quaternary and quinary sectors. So called experts, intellectuals, information technologists, chief executive officers, civil and political executives have failed to chart, regulate and control socio economies leading to declines in growth and development. The quaternary and quinary sectors have proved ineptitude, parasitic and self centred. They draw on huge salaries, bonuses, perks, privileges and creature comfort leaving socio economic institutions bankrupt. Huge budget deficits are attributed to payments towards their up keep. This has proved that nothing in life is certain, in spite of the existence, and presence, of the quaternary and quinqry experts, intellectuals and information technologists. In fact these people have become a risk, barrier and problem to socio economic growth and development. They add no value, but misery to the socio economic system and business organisation.

Lewis's Dual Sector Model of Development: The Theory of Trickle Down

Sir William Arthur Lewis (1915- 1991) was a Saint Lucian economist, with dual British citizenship. Lewis was well known, and knighted, for his immense contribution in the field of socio economic development. When Ghana became independent in 1957, Lewis became the country's first economic adviser, helping to draw up its first Five Year Development Plan (1959 – 1963). In 1959 he was appointed Vice Chancellor of the University of West Indies. In 1970, Lewis became director of the Caribbean Development Bank. To cap an illustrious career, he won in 1979, with Theodore Schultz, the Nobel Memorial Prize in Economics.

Lewis was an academic, professional and a practitioner in socio economic development and education. He was a West Indian (Black person) who directly experienced, and understood, the dialectics of colonial occupation economics and geo politics.

His key works are the Dual Sector Model, and the Theory of Economic Growth. The Lewis Model centred on a published article entitled 'Economic Development with Unlimited Supplies of Labour'. In this influential paper, he introduced what came to be called the Dual Sector Model, or the Lewis Model. In this work, Lewis combined an analysis of the historical experiences of developed countries with the central ideas of the classical economics, to produce a broad picture of the development process.

In his analysis, a capitalist sector develops by taking labour from a non capitalist backward 'subsistence' sector. At an early stage of development, there would be available an 'unlimited' supply of labour from the subsistence economy; which means that the capitalist sector can expand without the need to raise wages. This results in higher returns which are then re-invested in further capital accumulation. In turn the increase in capital stock leads the capitalists to expand employment by drawing further labour from the subsistence sector. As time goes by, the process becomes self sustaining, and leads to modernisation and economic development, though lop-sided.

The point at which the excess labour in the subsistence sector is fully absorbed into the modern sector, further capital accumulation begins to increase wages is called the Lewis turning point. The Lewisian turning point has recently gained credence, and circulation, in the contexts of China, India and South East Asia. (Bloomberg, 2010). Migrant labour flows to the north confirm Lewis' theory of dual sector socio economic development, driven by a combination of curiosity and practical need.

Another important off shoot of Lewis' theory of development is the trickle down process. Trickle down is the process when the economic gains from economic growth pass down throughout the society, eventually giving rise to development. (Leeson and Nixson, 2004). Lewis's theory attempted to address the challenges of development in less developed countries, as far back as 1954. The theory was based on the assumption that many LDCs had dual economies with both the traditional agricultural sector and a semi industrial sector. The traditional agricultural sector was viewed to be of a subsistence nature characterised by low productivity, low incomes, low savings and high under employment. The industrial sector was seen to be rather technologically developed, with some measure of investment, operating in an urban environment.

Lewis suggested his theory as solution to less developed countries. There should be aggressive development of urban industrialisation programmes through direct investment by external investors. These industrial firms would naturally offer higher wages than incomes from traditional agriculture. This would lead to migration from rural areas to urban centres. Urban areas would grow increasing demand for accommodation, consumer goods and services resulting in more employment. This would in turn free the rural areas of large populations. Indeed the amount of food and other resources available to the remaining rural folk could be shared amongst fewer people. This might generate surpluses which could be sold to generate income. Those who would have moved into urban areas would enjoy increased incomes, whilst those remaining in rural areas would have enhanced incomes. This would be a win, win situation. Savings from both systems would lead to investment eventually resulting in development.

Lewis saw savings and investment as the keys to development. As the savings from urban and rural settings increased so would windows of investment opportunities and entrepreneurship. Hence, a growing industrial sector would provide the incomes that could be spent and saved. This would in itself generate demand and also provide funds for investment. So income generated by the industrial sector would trickle down through out the economy benefiting all.

A good example is China's model of development. Satellite urban centres especially in the south, near sea ports, have sprouted to produce consumer goods mainly for export. This has meant that millions of people have moved to theses urban centres resulting in rises in incomes, and savings. An urban middle class is fast emerging, with rises in incomes and desire for certain goods leading to more investment ventures to satisfy the demand. All this, coupled with aggressive export drive, has led to increases in income and savings.

Limitations of the Lewis Model

Though there is the trickle down effect in countries like China, there have emerged new problems. Housing has been a problem with attendant problems of squalid living conditions, high cost of living consuming a big slice of the incomes. Because comparatively few people have remained to grow rice in the paddy fields acute shortages of rice have led to huge imports of wheat. Demand for goods has dropped world wide because of recession. This may lead to unemployment, fall in incomes and savings.

Rural to urban migration in less developed countries has been far larger than the industrial sector could provide employment. This has resulted in shanty dwellings, squalid living conditions, high cost of living, high rates of crime and destitution. Urban poverty has replaced rural poverty.

Besides, higher incomes do not necessarily lead to savings and investment. People are known to spend their incomes on consumer durables, expendables, luxury goods and non essential items. Countries, especially less developed ones, may spend resources on luxury buildings, executive aircraft, luxury cars, expensive travel and shopping sprees in metropolitan cities, instead of development projects. In the meanwhile essential infrastructure such as water, sewer reticulation, power generation and industrial manufacturing are non existent or dilapidated.

The industrial sector does not necessarily need increases in labour. It may be cost effective to invest in technology than rely on less efficient and less reliable labour. Due to less demand for goods produced, an industrial firm may scale down operations, or close down leading to retrenchments.

Harrod, Roy. F and Domar, Evsey: The Business Cycle and Economic Growth Model

This basic growth model was developed, independently, by Harrod and Domar in the 1930's. The British economist Sir Roy Harrod expanded upon earlier economic theories to develop his theory. Harrod relied on the work by John Keynes. Around the same time, the Russian, Evsey Domar came up with a similar model of economic growth on his own. The two joined forces to further develop new policies to encourage economic growth. According to the model there are thre kinds of growth, namely, warranted growth, actual growth, and natural rate of growth. Warranted growth rate is the rate of growth at which the economy does not expand indefinitely, or go into recession. This helps to explain actual factors that cause economic boom or doom. The model implies that economic growth depends on policies to increase investment, by increasing savings, and using that investment more efficiently through technological advances. The theory concludes that an economy does not find full employment and stable growth rates naturally. Hence, there is the need to intervene with actual rates of growth.

The Harrod-Domar Model is a macroeconomic theory that is used in development economics to explain an economy's growth rate in terms of the level of productivity of capital and saving. The theory is also used to measure the economic growth of a country as a whole. Under this model, the growth of the economy is calculated as a factor of capital production and the individual savings rate. Economists rely on the theory as one method of estimating long term economic growth rates. Combined with other models and theories, this calculation can provide valuable insights into the state of the economy. It may help policy makers develop new policies to encourage growth.

The theory was initially developed to help analyse the business cycle. It was later adapted to explain economic growth, or lack of it. The business cycle involved labour (persons with skills, expertise), using production factors (capital: raw materials, funds, machinery, equipment) leading to goods and services for sale. Incomes from the sales would lead to savings and investment. Investment would start the whole cycle resulting ultimately to sustained development. Breaks, inefficiency and failure in the chain of cycle would result in under performance, in productivity, and ultimately development. The logic of their arguments is that an economy's growth rate should be read in terms of the level of saving and productivity of capital. Economic growth rates depend on two things, that is, on the levels of savings with higher savings enabling higher investment levels. The main prediction of the theory is that GDP growth is proportional to the share of investment spending in GDP. (Van Rijckeghem 1966).

In other words, economic growth depends on the quantity and quality of labour, capital, incomes, savings and investment. Less developed economies have quantity of labour but not quality in terms of skills, expertise and sophistication. They also lack capital resources that hold back economic growth and development. So, capital, through direct investment is essential to generate higher output and income. Hence the need to inject large doses of investment through loans and donations from outside the country is paramount. The key to economic growth is to expand the level of investment both in terms of fixed capital and human capital. To achieve this, policies are needed that encourage investment, productivity, savings; generate technological advances which enable firms to produce more output with less capital.

In short the theory is based on the assumption that funding for capital investment comes with money that has been saved, rather than spent. By putting more money into savings accounts and other instruments, citizens make more money available for investors to borrow. With this borrowed money, companies expand operations, purchase new equipment, or invest in new, more productive technologies.

But here lies one of the problems with the theory. Recent experiences with the 2008 collapse of banking institutions, financial markets and firms citizens' savings and investments were pulverised. So it is full hardy to expect dispossessed citizens and investors to put their savings with banks and financial institutions that have the history of going down with their savings, investments and pensions. .

Limitations of the model

In developing countries it is fallacious to expect people to save for investment and capital development. Savings are largely dependent on income levels and resource distribution. So it is near impossible to increase savings, surplus income without major socio economic changes to increase, or redistribute, income.

The theory assumes that economic growth and economic development are the same. Economic growth refers to an increase in a country's output of goods and services. It is usually measured by changes in real GDP. Although economic growth is necessary it is not a sufficient condition of economic development. Economic development is the process of improving the quantity and quality of people's lives within a country taking into consideration composite indicators such as disposable income, life expectancy, nutritional levels, levels of education, measures of health.

It is difficult to stimulate the level of domestic savings especially in the case of LDCs where incomes are low. Besides low income levels, lack of sophistication, and knowledge, regarding priorities for investment would mitigate against meaningful investment.

The theorists' advocacy for borrowings, to fill the gap caused by insufficient savings, causes debt repayment problems later. The presence of unearned large sums of money gives a sense of false security leading to expenditure on non essential programmes. The propensity to spend, rather than save and invest, is the major problem of growth and development in developing countries, especially in Africa.

Nyerere, Julius, Kambarage (1922-1999) Economic, Social and Political Development for Self Reliance

Nyerere propounded that economic, social and political systems inherited from colonialists were geared towards the subjugation and subservience of the colonised peoples. Colonial ideology and practice denigrated the African as having no economy, no social structure and no advanced political system. In their place they desired to create white washed Africans subservient to the needs and interests of the capitalist occupiers. Religion was subtly woven into the fabric of society. The colonial system gave rise to individualism, self centredness, and preference for individual interests rather than the needs of the group. Thus capitalism, in Nyerere's view, promoted competition rather than cooperation.

As President of Tanzania he was painfully aware of the levels of poverty in the country. He sought to guide Tanzania on principles that had roots in Tanzanian tradition and socio economic processes. His brand of socialism was to be coloured with Tanzania's socio economic realities. This is the essence, and basis, of Ujamaa. Ujamaa is KiSwahili meaning living and working together harmoniously, in groups. A term which not only emphasised the Africanness of his socialism, but which also encapsulated a development design that was first and foremost Tanzanian. It was the most dramatic expression of the realisation that political independence provides the basis for socio economic independence.

The theory is informed and directed by a keen sense of justice and love of people. It disparages colonialist exploitation, oppression, elitism, brute ambition, private benefit, self seeking entrepreneurship and social antagonism. So Nyerere's theory of development is a blend of humanitarian idealism and pragmatic realism. It is hinged on universal ideals of human kind and the basic needs of ordinary people. In short, his theory is essentially egalitarian, humanitarian grounded in African socio economics and culture. It should eventually lead towards the elimination of poverty, inequality, aquisitiveness and wide differentials in living standards.

Nyerere's point of view has a messianic vision of a free, independent, productive and just populace. All citizens should live full, productive and satisfying lives. It is a reconstruction of people's norms and values of dignity, respect, personal integrity, moral ethics and universal neighbourly love. In other words, it is a human centred and self directed development strategy aimed at total liberation. For Nyerere, liberation meant total freedom of body, mind and soul. Total liberation involved freedom from external constraints and freedom from internal chains. Complete freedom meant freedom to pursue and achieve self actualisation. This was holistic development.

In all this, Nyerere saw education as the key to solving development problems. Thus education would lead to self development and self reliance. The spirit and letter of education for self reliance would enfuse the whole nation through primary, adult, secondary and tertiary education. It would be taught, learnt, encouraged and spread through education. Education should be realistically oriented towards the genuine needs of the average person. Schools should introduce and cultivate positive attitudes towards work, relevant knowledge, skills and values appropriate for the country's social, economic and political contexts. Education for self reliance should endeavour to develop persons fully regardless of background, colour, gender and creed. Education for self reliance combined wisdom with humility, perceptive insight with charm, recognition of the significance of the plight of ordinary people at home and abroad. The theory was meant to make people perceive beyond material existence reaching into the eternal, universal values of being and reality.

Steps in Implementing Education for Self Reliance

Nyerere is regarded as a philosopher ruler who had the rare opportunity to formulate and design a development theory and implement it personally.

Step 1. All rural people were moved into centralised, viable villages (Service Centres) where proper housing, safe water, sanitation, electricity and social services were put in place. Health centres, community halls and schools were built.

Step 2 involved curricula that would remove the existing colonial education system of its elitist, egoistic structures and goals. Education would be made to serve the needs and interests of the community as a whole. Primary and adult education for all would become the major goal of education. They would be complete courses in themselves, not preparation for secondary education. So, universal education would become the target of national development. Secondary and tertiary education would be for a selected few since the country could not afford secondary and tertiary education for many. Salaries and remuneration would be rationalised to remove wide disparities. Examinations would also test personal attributes such as character, competence, work attitudes and perseverance.

Step 3 involved the designing of education with production programmes. For an agrarian economy agriculture based programmes would dominate in an effort to meet basic needs of mainly rural people. Positive traditional knowledge, skills, norms, values, wisdom and experiences formed the pillars of education for development. Other knowledge systems, skills and experiences would come in to blend with the African ones. This formed an integrated approach to development.

Step 4 concerned the implementation of the designed education for self reliance programmes that espoused production, hard work, efficient use of local resources so as to contribute meaningfully to local and national economy. Schools became a preparation for life. Schools, colleges and universities would develop as totally self sufficient and self reliant socio economic entities (a farm, workshop, production unit).

The over all goal of development was to make all people lead a life of self sufficiency, self employment by developing knowledge, skills and experiences together. In other words, education should result in maturity, full empowerment and responsibility. Education and development should form an integral partnership forged between production, socialist principles, political awareness and praxis.

Limitations of Nyerere's theory

Though Nyerere's theory attempted to align new ideas with African socio economic culture there are a number of criticisms made against it. It relied too heavily on education as the prime mover of change and development. Education is not the only cause of development. The conflict theorists would argue that education is only a part of the superstructure which is affected by more powerful infrastructure like economics, disproportionate ownership of means, forces and fruits of production.

The theory was externally driven by an authority who claimed to know what was best for other people. It was formulated and implemented from the top. The top down strategy leads to problems of lack of ownership of the programme, misunderstanding, wrong interpretation and resistance even from those who stand to benefit from it. Moving people into centralised villages faced resentment by many people so affected. They felt displaced from their roots.

Nyerere's approach to development relegated the average person to a peasant life of manual work, menial existence aimed at satisfying basic needs. A person cannot live by bread alone. Above all, life is not all agrarian. Selection for secondary and tertiary education became problematic since many would qualify for secondary and tertiary education but for restricted numbers. The artificial cut off led to bottlenecks that could be detrimental to development. It also meant that the majority of the Tanzanian people would be left out of global world of knowledge, skills, language and technological developments.

Machel, Samora, Moises (1933-1986) Obscurantismo and Development

Samora Machel was a revolutionary leader of independent Mozambique. He was the first president of Mozambique after a protracted war against Portugal, the then colonial master. The Mozambicans got moral and physical support from the Soviet Union. Hence, Samora's world view was strongly influenced by Marxist-Leninist ideology.

He was known for his strong opposition to colonialism, imperialism and neo colonialism. He said that neo colonialism would remain resolute long after the colonisers and imperialists were gone. From the remnants and colonial hang over would emerge obscurantismo. We will come to it later on. It is important to examine Samora's theory of development from two philosophical perspectives, namely, historical determinism and Marxist-Leninism.

Philosophers have argued, and will continue to argue, on the plausibility of historical determinism. The advocates of this view assert that history is not made by persons, but by inexorable forces, or irrevocable laws. If these forces, or laws, do not manifest themselves through one person, they will do so through another. Tolstoy asserted that great persons are but the labels that serve to give a name to an event and, like labels, they have the least connection with the event itself. The persons would simply be in the right place at the right time. Events such as revolutions, discoveries, epidemics, wars, shape the world, direct history, and not persons. These feed the ambitions of wise, or mad, persons. For history has shown that no one cheers more for the tyrants than those they enslave. Historians on the other hand tend to view history and events through the lens backwards, getting a distorted and misleading picture. In other words the forces and hand of determinism are always at play.

However, Schlesinger (1987) pointed out that anyone who vigorously accepted a determinist view of life would have to abandon all notions of human intervention in events and social processes, and human responsibility, since it is unfair to praise or punish people for acts which are beyond their control.

However, determinists insist that persons occupy positions of authority not by choice but by invisible forces or laws. Out of this view came the process and practice of colouring, obscuring and darkening the knowledge, reality and world of the few who were meant to rule. This practice became known as obscurantism.

Plato glorified the practice by advocating a special class in society that was endowed with certain virtues, knowledge and skills. Hence, it was necessary to keep the general populace oblivious of the knowledge, language, and skills that determine the governance of the nation state. He called it the noble lie. The philosopher king, or ruler, had to be dressed in special, artificial shroud of secrecy, power and authority. Institutions such as religion, socio economics and politics had to subscribe to the doctrine of obscurantism. Aristotle, Kant and others took it up and added mysticism and esoteric language to it.

Hegel, on the other hand, advocated that persons in authority have to account for their behaviour to the populace. They should be in office through popular choice. Karl Marx, like Hegel, vehemently criticised obscurantism. They argued for open, general approach to knowledge, skills and language to demystify socio economics, politics and religion for ordinary people, the proletariat. Karl Marx castigated the ruling class, that is, those who own the means and forces of production. He argued that the ruling class, and their sub-servant classes, developed obscurantism to justify their exploitative capitalist system. The common person should prevail over and above all this. This should lead to socialism and ultimately communism.

Lenin expanded Marx's thesis. He postulated that truth only reveals itself when one gives up all preconceived ideas about self and the world. He underlined that the main objective was to make every person own the means and forces of production. Through theory and praxis, the masses should take active part in unravelling the exploitative and oppressive capitalist system. In other words everyone should be taught the motives and purposes of obscurantism.

Machel, a vowed Marxist-Leninist, took the cudgel and applied obscurantism to colonial, imperialist and neo colonial occupation and exploitation. For Africa the oppression and exploitation were sharper, harsher and rougher. Racism permeated every facet of life worsening the plight of the African. To Samora, the colonial, imperialist and neo colonial institutions such as socio economics, politics, religion and education were direct instruments of oppression and exploitation. Colour (White) and origin (Europe) marked as a measure of everything good, admirable and fashionable. Everything the white person said and did was considered good and correct by the African. The sun seemed to rise from the white person's arse. Catch phrases like 'Yes Baas,' 'Ndiyo Bwana' turned acquiescence into the neo colonial Baaskap mentality. Language for education, communication, politics, commerce, industry, and religion became that of the coloniser. African socio culture, knowledge, religion and ways of thinking were regarded as backward, primitive and barbaric. However, Samora disparaged some of Africa's socio cultural beliefs, such as witchcraft, irrational belief in supernatural practices, oppression of women, tribalism, looting and raiding expeditions, made obscurantismo take deeper roots. The colonialist encouraged Africans to be involved in rain making ceremonies, or Christian praying sessions, for rain instead of drilling boreholes in dry regions. Because of neo colonialism, the post colonial Africa is plagued with problems of development. So for Samora, obsurantismo is a big barrier to economic growth and development. (Machel, 1982).

Political independence was the first essential step to African liberation. But to stop there was like building the first span of a bridge, and sitting on it, while claiming that the river has been crossed. The struggle for socio economic independence should fall on the shoulders of everyone. Africa needs unity, for freedom, peace, and a chance to develop to its full socio economic potential. There should be free flow of trade, commerce, industry, communication and people across all borders. Samora advocated for a socio economic United States of Africa that would make Africa harness its huge resources to the benefit of its populace. Separately individual states would be weak and vulnerable in a jungle of international trade and finance. Because African states as individuals would be the weakest creatures in that jungle, they would be exploited mercilessly and set upon with impunity by the strongest creatures. Africans would as a result, pay dearly in money, freedom, resources, debt and poverty. So Machel advocated for African unity in order for Africa to develop fully.

On education, Samora suggested a four stage economic growth and development strategy. The first stage is to embark on an aggressive education and re-education process for the populace to eradicate neo colonialism, customs and beliefs that hinder growth and development. Education should, as a matter of priority, emphasise modern and progressive knowledge bases, scientific approaches to agricultural, commercial, and industrial production.

The second stage is targeted at school curricula that should develop a new awareness, a consciousness that liberates the mind from the shackles of neo colonialism and obscurantismo. Primary, secondary and tertiary education should inculcate values of combining theory and practice, self sustaining programmes, leading to self sufficiency.

The third stage involves universities, colleges, commerce and industry being linked. They should aim at scientific production of goods and services. Good, sound education should produce people who add value to life, and not add suffering and misery to it. The fourth, but very important stage, is the production of a revolutionary cadreship of all the populace, based on equality, fairness, integrity, hard work and social justice. For Machel, empowered lives lead to resilient nationals.

Limitations of Machel's Theory of Development

The major limitation of the theory is that he based it on Marxist-Leninist ideology which is alien and an importation from the north. Marxist-Leninism with its esoteric aims, values and language, is strange to the African. Machel could be accused of bringing on the African yet another form of obscurantismo. Nyerere would argue for a home-grown, comprehensible ideology compatible with African socio culture.

Another problem with the theory is that there are few success stories of Marxist-Leninist nation states. The Soviet Union disintegrated leaving Russia entering the capitalist route. Maoist-Leninist China has abandoned the ideology by embracing western modes of production and its US dollar currency. China has gone into Africa to ruthlessly exploit Africa's resources with an insatiable appetite. Besides, aid from Marxist-Leninist states has been limited to arms, weapons and snow ploughs. To make matters worse for African states with limited resources, western nations and donors have been reluctant to fund projects in countries espousing Marxist- Leninism.

Machel's theory is a top down development strategy that denies people ownership of ideology, projects and programmes.

All the above notwithstanding, Machel's theory of development helps us to unravel, and analyse the intricacies, workings, hidden motives, exploitative nature of capitalism, imperialism and neo colonialism. We should, in particular, guard against obscurantismo in subtle and overt forms of corruption, nepotism, racism, sectarianism and intolerance. All this makes us understand and appreciate how neo colonial hang- overs and machinations of imperialism hinder Africa's development.

Ngugi wa Thiong'o (1986) warns against neo colonialism, imperialism and capitalism. He says there is no area of African lives that has not been affected by the social, political and expansionist wants and interests of western capitalism. These range from that of the very reluctant Africans, driven by whip and gun to work on the cotton plantations of America, the rubber plantations in the Congo, the gold and diamond mines in Southern Africa, to that of the present African workers spending their meagre hard earned income on imported cars and other goods like razor blades and coca cola. All this bolsters the same western industries that got off on the loot and plunder of the continent. Societies in Africa have grown against the gory background of western imperialism and its shifting manifestations of slavery, colonialism and neo colonialism.

Hence, socio culture in Africa has grown against the same stunting, suffocating and dwarfing back drop. Nationalist governments in Africa show obscurantismo in terms of misplaced development. There are signs of progress without development. African governments' propensity for showiness and extravagance proliferate. Africans have a flair for expensive and prestigious projects. They indulge in big stadiums, huge hotels, state mansions, burial museums, statues, presidential jets and limousines, when people wallow in abject poverty. No dividends are earned from such large misplaced investments. This is typical obscurantismo as the African leaders vie to out do, and out shine, the colonialist masters and their mistresses.

The present Africans have become a caricature, a parody of the colonial socio culture. The difference between the coloniser and the colonised is the same. Obscurantism has made the affected people feel, and behave, more than hybridised creatures. In other words they are worse …they are genetically modified socially, economically and psychologically.

Questions for review

What lessons can you draw from any one of the theories covered in this chapter? Nyerere talks of home grown strategies for national development, discuss the merits and demerits of such strategies. What would you consider to be the limitations of Machel's theory of obscurantismo?

Economic growth refers to an increase in a country's out put of goods and services. It is usually measured by changes in real gross domestic product (GDP). Economic growth is caused by improvements in the quantity and quality of the factors of production that a country has available. The most important ones are land, capital, labour and enterprise. These are also referred to as engines of development. Conversely, economic decline occurs if the quantity and quality of these engines of development fall.

Improving the Quantity and Quality of Land Resources

Land covers the earth and on it we find critical resources like soil, water, minerals, roads, rail, air ports, water ports, buildings, fauna and flora. Without land life on earth will almost be impossible. So land should be managed prudently and efficiently, otherwise development suffers resulting in life extinction. Civilizations such as Egypt, Sumeria, Peru, Greece and Rome thrived on prudent use of land resources and technology. Agriculture, construction, mining, manufacturing, transportation and communication depend on land resources. If not managed properly and efficiently this can lead to lack of development.

Land is a finite resource in that it does not stretch. It can deteriorate in quantity and quality. Together with its resources it can be expended. So a country's level of development is determined by the quantity and quality of its land resources.

Improving the Quantity and Quality of Capital Resources

Capital refers to human made resources such as machinery, factories, buildings, technology, plants, money and goods. Measures of availability, quantity, quality, flows in and out of a country tell whether a country is developed or not. Capital flight, that is, the movement of capital resources out of a country in response to unfavourable domestic circumstances can lead to serious socio economic problems.

There are two forms of capital. Direct productive capital includes factory, plant and equipment, expert, technology, finance and investor. Indirect or facilitating capital involves arteries of development such as roads, rail, air and water ports, bridges, power grids, fuel depots.

Energy sources are critical engines of socio economic growth and development. Electric power is an essential aspect of development. So a country's generating capacity and sustainability become top priority. Safe, renewable, green and environment friendly energy sources are imperative. Where there is abundance of water, like in tropical regions, hydro electric power is cheap, safe and clean. Geo thermal power generation, though expensive to drill the wells, is clean and sustainable. Volcanic active areas like the East African Rift Valley, are ideal sources of geo thermal renewable energy. Africa is sitting on abundant sources of energy.

Solar power can be available in most parts of the world. Though it needs higher capital outlay, once it is installed it provides continuous electric power. Solar photovoltaic array (SPV) comes from the basic element converting sunlight into electricity through a solar cell made out of silicon material. A solar cell generates 0.6 volts open circuit. To have building block of practical use, 36 identical cells are connected in series to make a module suitable for charging a 12 volt battery. By putting them in series and parallel arrangement, the required current power levels can be generated. The sunlight produces SPV array providing direct current that is inverted to alternating current for use in ordinary appliances. The power needed during daylight, and night time requires storage in a bank battery. Photo voltaic electricity can be used to drive water pumps, light homes, schools and factories, power computers, internet, television, cell phones and other accessories.

Improving the Quantity and Quality of Human Resources

Human resources fall into a number of categories. These range from technologists, experts, managers, artisans, technicians to general workers. Human capital, that is, the accumulated skills, knowledge and expertise of personnel, is critical to the success of production. It is not just the quantity of but the quality of personnel. This depends on the educational provision in a country, the relevance and level of content, knowledge, skills and motivation.

Investment spending on human capital involves opportunity cost that should be balanced in terms of current consumption. Hence, expenditure on education and training should have socio economic benefits. It is prudent to spend more on production than human capital development. It is not the level and amount of education that is needed for a country's socio economic growth. Rather it is the presence of entrepreneurial, enterprising and risk taking individuals that creates windows of opportunities for economic growth. There is need for a people, a leadership that has the strength to turn moments of adversity into opportunity. The presence of a people, a leadership is necessary that has the wisdom to see further than the ordinary eye can see, and the courage to challenge conventional thinking and worn ideas. There is need for a people who are prepared to reinvent the economy to seize the future. There is need for a leadership that can shape individual and collective destinies through hard work, honest dealing, personal responsibility, optimism and hope.

In short, the development of inventors, innovators, developers, technologists and sophisticated professionals leads to socio economic growth. Examples are Japan, Germany, United States of America, United Kingdom, Taiwan and Singapore. Reliance on Multinational Corporations and foreign driven programmes can lead to lack of enterprise culture. So efforts should be made to provide enterprising and entrepreneurial education and training for local people in a country.

The Role, Power and Place of Investment in Socio economic Development

The process of acquiring capital is called investment. The level and quality of investment directly affect the level of economic development. Foreign direct investment through individuals and companies can stimulate a country's economic activity. The efficiency and effectiveness of the labour force depends on the education, amount and quality of capital they have.

Investment Portfolios and Strategies

Research and practice have shown that the world owes a lot to enterprising people. Examples are persons in ancient Egypt who invented and developed writing, the alphabet, numbers, paper, ink, wheel and axle, mathematics for construction. Today we have micro wave technology, space travel, satellite innovations that have transformed our lives. These persons invest their time, energy, resources and brains in activities that benefit both the individual and nation. Some people say that they are born not made. But enterprise can be learnt especially by observing difficult situations. Problems propel certain persons to activate their brains for creativity. So exposing people, especially the young, to solving problems helps towards the development of skills in entrepreneurial skills. Creativity is regarded as the mother of invention and innovation. Ideas can be turned into income generating activities.

In economic development, investment can be the preserve of certain individuals with a knack for seeing windows of opportunity and use them to stimulate the economy. These are persons who make things happen. It is said that there are three types of people: those who make things happen; those who watch things happen; and those who wonder what has happened.

The Meaning of the Term Investment

Investment is the purchase of capital for production. It is the process of acquiring capital. It can also refer to purchase, as changes occur in stocks and shares. Investment is in two main parts. Net investment is where individuals or companies acquire new machinery, build new plants and factories. This type of investment adds value to the capital stock of the economy. The other type is called replacement investment where individuals or companies replace obsolete or inefficient machinery, plants, factories and technology. The level and quality of investment directly affect the level and quality of economic growth. Portfolio is a set of investments owned by an individual or company. The major function of investment portfolios is to ensure streams of income for the individual, group or nation. It can range from stocks and shares, precious metals, to buildings. It is as if an individual or company is carrying a flat leather case containing papers and documents pertaining to investments owned. Portfolio is also used to refer to an individual's or company's assets.

Asset is a thing or property that has value and can be used to pay for goods, services, or sold to settle debts. The term asset stripping is usually used in commerce to describe the unscrupulous practice of buying at cheap price an individual's or company's assets, with financial difficulties, and then selling the assets individually to make a profit. Investment portfolios have their strengths and weaknesses. So it is prudent to have a variety of them.

Real Estate or Fixed Assets

The safest is real estate, also referred to as fixed assets. Real estate includes productive land, buildings, infrastructure such as rail, road, ports, bridges, dams, power plants and grids. These are of a permanent nature and can be used to produce goods and services, rent or lease out, back debts as security. There are many factors to consider in real estate investing: area of property (urban, periphery, rural), type of property (commercial, residential), present and future trends (economic, industrial).

But in cases of crises, like war, one cannot move with them to safer destinations. Rogue laws and practices by governments can dispossess the owners of their fixed assets.

So current assets, also called consumer durables, may come in handy. These include livestock, vehicles, machinery, furniture, valuables and human resources. These can be moved in case of need. But this is their main weakness given wrong hands, thieves and robbers. So the Old Mutual organisation's investment strategy pays dividends. Old Mutual work on the interplay between an individual, or group, make money, the money should buy property, and property should generate funds for the individual or group. The complete cycle of job, money, property creates wealth. The Old Mutual policy is summarised as: individual at work, money at work and property at work. One can never go wrong in terms of investment.

Job and Employment

One's job is an asset and an investment. Finance, time, effort and postponement of gratification go into human resource development and training at the individual, family, national and international levels. So as an individual, a working person is one of the biggest asset-producing the most income in the family portfolio.

Some jobs are riskier than others. No job is that safe. Jobs can be lost through retrenchment, redundancy, perceived inefficiency and lack of productivity. Jobs can fail to pay dividends through poor remuneration, worthless currency, inefficient management of resources or just incompetence. Not even the highest person in the organisation or government has a safe job. Things can change on a heart beat. So a job can be counted on both sides as fixed income or equity. (Boldrin and Levine, 2001).

Equity is ordinary stocks and shares that carry no fixed or reliable interest. Hence, there is need to rely on portfolios that are safer.

Benefit Plans as an Investment

Benefit plans hedge against the unforeseen such as job loss, illness or even death. Pension, health, accident and death insurance plans help to cushion individuals, and groups, against unforeseen circumstances. But the major weaknesses of benefit plans are that they depend on the integrity of the insurer. One has to rely on what one is given. One does not have ready access to the money. Socio economics like inflation and devaluation can play havoc with the benefit funds. All these can lead to difficulties and even destitution.

Stocks and Shares

Another form of investment is stocks and shares which belong to what is sometimes called casino economics. It is regarded as gambling with one's money. Stocks and shares are volatile and speculative. One's money can disappear without trace with no answers given. Companies can go down despite their knowledge, confidence and previous track records. Banks and countries can collapse without notice. Examples of countries, together with their financial institutions, that have gone bankrupt are the European nations dubbed PIIGS, namely Portugal, Italy, Ireland, Greece, Spain. Stocks and shares are not worth what one thinks they are worth. They are worth what how much someone else is willing to pay for them. Besides, most company shares suffer liquidity problems. They can become completely illiquid. These investment portfolios should come low on one's asset allocation. However, some people have made fortunes on stocks and shares. Their performance on the stock market must be constantly monitored so as to sell when they are high, or to buy when they are low. Skill is needed in this financial game.

A safer alternative is to purchase bonds, not shares, in a company that shows a profitable future. So, one becomes a bond holder, not a share holder. An example would be to invest in assets related to the American natural gas (shale) and oil industry, in particular, its infrastructure such as liquefied natural gas (LNG) construction, terminal ports and containers, transportation through pipelines and shipping tankers. EXXON, a gas and oil company, has tradition and facilities to do that. EXXONMOBIL also have perfected the art of horizontal drilling and hydraulic fracking that are critical to natural gas mining. America is sitting on vast resources of natural gas and oil just discovered. By the year 2017 America is going to be the world's leading producer and exporter of LNG and oil. So buying into assets in form of bonds and royalties in companies there pays enormous dividends with no risk to the investment. Even when a company goes bankrupt one would still benefit from sales of assets, infrastructure, and possible future re-organisation of the same, or formation of a new company.

It is also prudent to buy assets, via bonds, in up market technology based companies such as Sony Electronics, Su-kam Power systems, Siemens, JDS Uniphase High band Width, Cree Research Company LEDs, Bloomberg Chemical Industries. The future lies with these, science, technology and innovation based firms. It is worth investing in them. A recent development on the stock exchange such as the New York Stock Exchange is royalty interests bundled into vehicles listed and traded, even on line. One can buy and sell them just like regular stock. So owning royalty interests is a valuable asset that allows one to collect money, year after year, with no risk, and further costs. Besides buying royalties in gas and oil companies one can buy them in Apple, Google, Bank of America creating lucrative royalty income stream.

Precious Commodities

One of the oldest, and safest, investment portfolio is in precious commodities such as gold, silver, diamonds, sapphires and emeralds. These valuables can protect one from financial crises. Gold is not money but a store of value. It does not suffer from diminished returns. It is not used up. There are a number of investment strategies one can use, as an individual or company. One can buy gold bars or bullion kept in a safe or bank. One can buy gold coins, for example, Canadian Maple Leaf, American Eagle, South African Kruger Rand. Another way is to invest in mines producing and selling gold. The trick is to go for a company that has vast gold deposits in million grams or ounces, has built a mine and is extracting gold. Gold stocks can be bought online from reputable firms like Yamana Gold Toronto, European Goldfields, Arizona Star, Resource Corp.

Another way of investing in gold is to buy bundles of royalties from gold mining companies. The investor shares in the income accrued by the company. By investing in royalties, the investor avoids all the normal risks of doing business, and paid over and over for owning a valuable asset. One's only investment is in the ownership of the valuable asset, the gold mine or field. So the trick is to invest in a precious mineral industry where demand and profits are certain to go up. This industry produces such an asset that has retained its value and purchasing power for all recorded human history.

Gold is a universally recognised store of value. Its natural properties have imbued the element with traits that humans find intrinsically valuable, and well suited to use as a form of exchange. It is durable, portable, divisible, and does not corrode. It could be the best hedge against inflation, uncertainty, and financial crises. Demand and profit is partly guaranteed by socio cultures in China, India and many countries in Asia. Two thirds of the world's population reside there.

Companies to purchase bundles of royalties from could be Newmont Mining, Goldstrike Mines, Barrick Gold (ABX). Gold royalty investment yields returns that are much higher, and above all, it is acquiring a right into the income from company. One collects a percentage of the income from operations of a company, year after year, by remote control as it were.

Sansberry & Associates Resource (2012) note that, it is prudent to invest in silver. Silver is real money and is used in coin minting. It is also a versatile mineral that is used in manufacturing and gem industry. So it is expendable, hence, demand rises. Silver is much cheaper than gold so one can buy as much as possible for sale as demand rises. More than 95% of silver goes into industry. Silver is used in many things such as health care, food industry, cell phones, batteries, green technologies, fabrics that are odour resistant, energy efficient windows, compact discs. When silver is used for industrial and technological purposes it is gone and cannot be reused. So there are no stock piles in the world. There are only 20 companies that mine silver in the world. Over 90% of all the silver that has been mined in the last 5000 years has gone from supply. On the other hand, most of the gold produced in the same period is still around in one form or another. That is the unique investment opportunity for silver. It can be one of the safest, most lucrative investments of the future. Methods, sources and strategies for investment in silver are the same as for gold.

The table below shows the significance of gold and precious minerals as an all time investment portfolio. It is not too often that we see a major shift within the precious metals market. The last such recalibration in sentiment for precious metals investors was the introduction of gold and silver ETF in 2004, and the subsequent explosion in exchange traded products (ETPs) for bullion and precious metals equities.

It is illustrating to show the precious metals' market performances using the Rock and Stock statistics below.

Rock and Stock Statistics

	2012	**One month ago**	**One year ago**
Gold	1 737.00	1 766.75	1 652.50
Silver	32.33	34.65	31.97
Platinum	950. 25	964.33	860.00
Copper	3.75	3.83	3.25
Oil	92.10	94.98	86.11
Gold Producers (GDX)	51.73	54.79	53.55
Gold Junior Stocks (GDXJ)	23.64	25.22	28.36
Silver Stocks (SIL)	24.47	25.34	28.36
Toronto Stock Exchange (TSX)	12 415.98	12 436.52	11 849.50
TSX Venture	1 315.62	1 343.52	1 525.82

Casey Research, 2012

New Trends in Investment

Investment in gold and precious mineral portfolios is critical to withstanding the likely fallout ahead from the mountain of un payable government debt and politically promised benefits. The second reason is that there is an impending dismal failure of all major currencies, especially the US dollar's inexorable decay in purchasing power. So, investors have to shift from paper (promissory notes) to the physical, that is, real estate, precious metals and other strategic commodities. The third reason is that there is uncertainty in global economic, political, fiscal and monetary policies. The world is moving from recession to depression. Other issues of concern relate to complicated custodial structures, leasing or substituting paper certificates (ETPs) for physical metal such as gold and silver bars. Gold is one of the world's best, time tested form of investment. Having precious metal in one's control, and at one's disposal, empowers one in times of turmoil and crisis. Hence, the World Gold Council predicts a sustained surge in gold and precious metals production. Prudent investors are moving to Hard Assets Alliance storage locations in Zurich, London, New York Salt City, Melbourne, the Vatican and Singapore. An investor can conduct all purchases and services online. The metal is fully allocated, registered in the investor's name and given full security and confidentiality. Buying, selling and taking delivery is easy and user friendly. Linked to this form of investment is a network of dealers who compete for business thus ensuring best available prices. Let us move to investment in diamonds and other gems.

Diamonds and other gems are used in crowns, rings, neck laces and bracelets. They have intrinsic and universal value. Individuals tend to invest in them since they can be disposed in times of need. Asian women of means move around as precious mineral portfolios. The adornments are more than mere decoration. But this area of investment has its risks such as theft and robbery. Since gems have only intrinsic value problems in the economies can devalue their potential as financial hedge.

Rare and precious artefacts and antics such as paintings, pictures, articles, stamps, and coins can make a fortune for collectors, sellers and buyers. This is another form of investment one has to look around for. Many a family, or home, carry valuable artefacts that can bring in a small fortune. One needs to check with experts in antics and auctioneers before disposing of artefacts and antics.

Though investments in jewellery, coins and artefacts held by individuals offer a layer of economic protection, robbery, abduction and theft are possible threats to fortune, limb and life. So these should be kept, under insurance cover, with safe havens like banks.

Even gold or silver bullion and stocks have risks. So the investor has to diversify investment portfolios, geographically, politically and economically. As a matter of fact all forms of investment need diversification. The remedy is to internationalise investment portfolios. This reduces four possible primary risks.

As bankrupt governments get increasingly desperate assets held domestically could be a target for confiscation. A government with unbearable debt and unfunded liabilities burden can invoke confiscation laws. The United States government in 1933 invoked the FD Roosevelt Gold confiscation law, the executive order which forced delivery of citizens' gold and silver in exchange for cash. So all gold and silver held by financial institutions and individuals were compulsorily acquired for national interest and survival. Other examples abound in developing countries. Conflicts and strife such as wars and insurrections can reduce investments to nought.

Another area of risk is capital controls. Capital controls can be used to limit, or eliminate a citizen's ability to carry, or remit money abroad. So all investments would be trapped inside the country, and would be at the mercy of taxing and regulating schemes by the authorities. Although one might leave the country, one's assets cannot travel with one. These administrative actions, and asset seizures by government agencies, without notice or due process, leave the victim without means of legal defence. All this leads to lack of personal control and helplessness.

So having assets held elsewhere adds to one's options when crises arise. One will have a source of funds available for survival, business, entrepreneurial pursuits, investment, or pleasure. But it is essential for one to understand conditions and complying requirements in the investment destination. Foreign held assets require caution, research, greater awareness, planning and management. All the same geographic, political and economic diversity of asset location is an essential strategy against an uncertain future.

The Mainz Income Stream Investment (Casey Research, 2014)

This form of investment has roots in economic history. The Guttenberg Press, which was invented in Mainz, Germany, is considered to have made collecting regular income, as royalty, possible. It allowed book publishers, and authors, to make money after creating a valuable piece of work. A good example today is President Barack Husein Obama who makes $72 000 a month from sales of his best selling book: The Audacity of Hope. The Mainz investment remains one of the greatest, yet safest ways to get a good return. One makes an investment, or controls a valuable asset, and gets paid over and over; while somebody else takes the risks of printing, developing, publishing, marketing and distributing.

Other forms of investment in this lucrative portfolio, lie in owning a patent, on drugs, songs, recording and films. So, by investing in patents and royalties, the investor collects streams of income for owning a valuable asset.

Instead of owning a patent one could become a part owner of a popular trademark. Examples of trademarks are fast food chains A&W, McDonalds, Burgar King. Every time one of these 1 000 food outlets sells a burger, shake or fries, one collects royalties. It is similar to celebrities using popular brands like Nike, Rolex, Omega, and getting paid for advertising the product and its trademark. This investment opportunity gives one a 3% royalty on all sales the trademark company makes. Royalties are payable monthly, quarterly or yearly.

There is also a stock market opportunity in the music business that allows one to own part of the rights to royalties from a catalogue of over 35 000 copyrighted songs. Classic works by Bing Crosby, Duke Ellington, Jim Reeves, Percy Sledge, Elvis Presley, The Beatles, The Beach Boys, Clarence Carter, Steve Wonder, Yvone Chaka Chaka, Louis Armstrong, Hugh Masekela, Miriam Makeba and Sam Mangwana, make enormous sales. Every time one of these 35 000 songs is played on the radio, television, in movies or advertisements, the investor collects royalties.

Money, Currency or Cash as Investment

The least safe form of investment is in currency, money or cash. These have wings. They are open to the vagaries of liquidity, inflation and devaluation. Currencies can be in cash or kind. They have been convenient means of exchange. In the 16th Century tulip bulbs were used as valuable currency in Europe. Their fragile and cumbersome nature led to the use of gold and silver coins produced by different groupings. Variations in mass, content and make made trade transactions difficult. Eventually their place was taken over by paper money printed against gold bullion held in the minting country's vaults. These promissory notes endeavoured to pay the bearer an equivalent sum worth in gold held by the minting authority. In time some promissory notes became more valuable and powerful than others. Other currencies have become less worth than the paper they are printed on.

Money allows people to exchange goods and services widely, greatly increasing the specialization of labour and production, and facilitating the socio economic competitive advantage. Money also plays the critical function of communications between, and among many, disparate actors. Through money price changes guide producers and consumers. But there ends the advantages of money. Whe money loses its value, it cannot be trusted. So the entire monetary system breaks down. The price signals cannot be relied upon. Then it becomes harder and harder for people to exchange labour and capital.

The next alternative is to turn to credit, that is, borrowing. Credit enables an economy to grow by facilitating the growth of capital and savings investment through real interest rates. But the problem is that very few people, if any, are willing to delay consumption and trust their savings in an economy that refuses to pay the savers any return above inflation for their savings. Moreover, borrowing often leads to a cal de sac, a dead end, where there is no way out. The debt trap leads to dire socio economic traits. So a country tries to avoid debt repayment by default by printing more money. For developing countries, printing money is akin to digging own socio economic grave. For those with the world's reserve currencies, like the USA, printing money can save them from debt default, and socio economic collapse, for some time. The USA is one of the few debtors in the world who can legally print their own currency, and push it into the market. Britain did it in the 1970's with the pound sterling, with delayed disastrous consequences.

Eventually, currencies such as the United States dollar, the British pound and the Japanese yen took economic centre stage. The advent of the US Petro -dollar made it the main exchange currency. Many countries kept US dollars in their vaults for payment of oil and other essential commodities. Because of the demand for US dollars the United States of America Federal Bank printed the currency wholesale. This helped America become a super power able to fund space exploration and external wars. Even with the advent of technological plastic money such as credit cards, the US dollar has reigned supreme for more than 30 years. (Levine, 2010). The US dollar forms the basis of the world's financial system. It is what banks around the world hold in reserve against their loans. At present the USA is the only country in the world that does not have to pay for its imports in a foreign currency. Others have to buy US dollars first, then, buy goods and services. So the people in the USA do not have to produce or export anything to get the dollars to purchase goods and services they require. All the USA had to do was to borrow and print more money, if need be. So the USA has afforded to be the world's largest debtor. The USA resorts to repaying its loans by printing trillions of new dollar notes. The US Federal Reserve Bank calls this printing process the QE, that is, quantitative easing. In 2013 they are on QE3 printing $85 billion a month. The USA has treasury issue bonds to the Federal Reserve Bank which issues a cheque to itself and proceeds to print dollars to be distributed by key banks after adding commissions. The printed dollar is not backed by any gold reserves.

However, this is bound to change because of events in the world. The world recession since 2008 has driven economies to safer investment portfolios like gold, silver and other precious minerals. Investors quickly, and quietly, move into hard assets such as land, buildings and precious metals. Real estate, especially commercial and industrial properties, has rallied to hedge against bankruptcy. Revolutions in the Arab world, the Arab spring, have brought on stage leaders who view the United States of America, and its dollar currency, as forces of imperialism and oppression. Iran, one of the biggest oil exporting countries in the world, has dumped the US Petrol dollar. They now exchange oil for technology to build refineries, nuclear powered plants, space technology and manufacturing plants. China, one of the biggest holders of the US dollar, is off-loading the dollar in exchange for physical commodities and technology. China is actively taking steps to phase out the US dollar as its reserve currency from its financial system. That means a third of the world's population is saying good bye to the US dollar.

Furthermore, the USA QE has left its creditors with a sour taste in the mouth as they feel cheated. So creditors, that is, foreign countries like China, companies, investors will either stop accepting US dollars in repayment, or greatly discount the value of the new US dollars. With the US dollar losing its value, and position as the world's currency, gas, oil, food, clothing, vehicles and machinery will become very expensive world wide. This will lead to run away inflation, citizens' protests, governments getting over thrown, resulting in civil strife. When a reserve currency collapses, everything else goes with it: markets, stocks, bonds, commodities, derivatives and other investments since they are all priced in the reserve currency. Investors will be left with no choice but to go for strategic commodities such as real estate, gold, silver, base metals, oil leading to these commodity prices soaring. This flight of capital can lead to recession and eventually world depression.

This could be the end of the US dollar as a major currency player on the world economic field. Investors holding the US dollar as investment will go down the economic drain with it. Stocks and shares, insurance schemes and other securities in US dollar are in danger of pulverising.

This is what happens when countries get too far into debt, or when they consume too much and produce too little. Socio economic history tends to repeat itself. Britain's pound sterling was the reserve currency for most of the world for 200 years, throughout the 18th and 19th centuries. But because of massive expenditure as a result of government take over major industries and social welfare Britain got broke, and went into debt. The Bank of England resorted to printing money. With it, went the pound, making way for the US dollar to enter world trade as reserve currency.

But it may not be all doom and gloom. Socio economic history has shown resilience. The International Monetary Fund is advocating for a new global world reserve currency created by the World Bank and supervised by the IMF.

Governments are now realising that solutions to deficits and debt crises lie in drastically reducing costs, cutting spending, living within one's means, and removing anti business laws. .

The above notwithstanding, the US dollar may resurge as world currency number one because of new vast discoveries of natural gas, shale gas, and oil. Technologies such as horizontal drilling and hydraulic fracking have revolutionised the gas and oil industry. America is sitting on vast resources of shale gas and oil, hitherto inaccessible. Estimates put it at 10 Gulf oil states put together. The Texas coast, Bakken/ Three Forks in North Dakota, and Montana have more than 20 big oil and shale formations, equivalent to 20 Persian Gulf fields. Goldman Sachs estimates that USA would outpace Saudi Arabia in oil and gas production before the end of this decade. Market Watch say, by 2017, America will be the world's largest producer and exporter of natural gas and oil.

This will catapult America to a super power, economically, politically and strategically. All major consumers of oil such as ships, power generating plants, trucking and hauling groups are fast converting to shale gas combustion. It is cheaper, cleaner and more efficient than oil and diesel. All this will entail massive local and global build-out of liquefied natural gas (LNG) infrastructure such as LNG terminals, special tankers and containers, shipping, natural gas turbines, engines and accessories. In other words, the oil and shale boom will become the greatest creation of wealth in America's history, given President Obama's (Obamacare) social security programmes and job creation schemes. The shift in oil wealth will be from the Middle East to the northern hemisphere, yet again.

But there are political movements that can make countries like USA and Britain regress socio economically. The 2017 president Trump Donald policies of closed door nationalism move the country from global lucrative economies to limited short sighted socio economic benefits. The 2016 British exit from the European common market has similar disastrous consequences for Britain. If China is prudent on quality of product it stands to benefit a lot from the Amexit and Brexit movements from the greater global socio economies. Russia under Putin Vladimir and his autocratic and authoritarian governance cannot take advantage of USA and British socio economic regressions.

A shrewd investor taps into the massive wealth in other America and globally. Companies in fluid engineering, LNG construction, LNG shipping, LNG terminals, chemical industries, natural gas driven turbines and engines will mushroom, raking in huge profits for at least two decades to come.

Closing Remarks on Investment Portfolios

We have seen that the field of investment portfolio, choice, destination and location needs careful research, planning and management just like life itself. For an unplanned investment portfolio is an unplanned life. It is important to also consider asset allocation before making any investment moves. It is worth one's life, and a country's development.

If investment is wrongly done, one can get totally hosed. That is not fair, one would say. But that is the truth, and a social fact. That is the way life works. For one who has the knowledge, go the spoils. Skill, prudence, insight, good judgement, and common sense, are essential in investment planning and decision making. Hence,

So besides the need for consultants one should develop by working hard on self empowerment learning to have diverse tools of life.

The Need for Diverse Tools of Life

Diverse and multipurpose tools of life are skills, attitudes, knowledge and motivation necessary for individual, group and national success, growth and development. The micro world builds the macro world. Micro refers to the individuals' private life and the macro refers to the community and world at large. So the following secrets of success, growth and development relate to both the micro and the macro world described above.

It is useful to start with Bernard Levine's (1997) exhortation. We are architects of our lives. We should create our own opportunities and make things happen. We should set ourselves specific goals and proactively monitor our progress. We should be of service by keeping doing good things for others without counting the cost. We must turn our defeats into victories. We should control our environment, and mix with the kind of people who inspire us. We should keep our attitude positive and our health in fine trim. In everything we do we should meditate and always plan constantly. For, indeed we are the magnets of our circumstances. Above all we should never give up. We should try, try and try again until we succeed.

The Forbes Rich and successful list underlines three important secrets, which could as well be read as commonsense. We should never be afraid to fail. Risk taking is not a gamble but a calculated risk. We should never allow failure and bad experience destroy optimism and passion for a development project. We should learn from mistakes and change course but not direction.

We should think critically by looking creatively at problems and new sources. We must look at problems from different angles. We should look for alternatives. Crises should lead to creativity. Great ideas flourish out of a crisis. So we should think positive and think possible.

And just like Levine, we are advised to never give up. We should persevere and not perish. We must try again and again till we reach the finishing line. We can start small, at the micro level and reach the macro level. The message for us here is hope, courage and determination. Once we choose hope and determination everything is possible, for the individual, community, nation and the world.

The Formula for Success.com put it succinctly. If we have no plan, that is planning for failure. We must be self starting, self correcting, innovative and organised. We must build on team work and avoid the blame culture. We should be fair, just, and honest. We must have collective responsibility and ownership of the project. So the catalyst for success lies in changing our mind set. We can change our lives. We should aspire to be great, creative, to achieve and succeed. There must be an active search for solutions. We should remember that we all make mistakes, but it is how to come out of it that matters. Those who do not make mistakes achieve nothing worth noting in life.

Great achievers move from intention to impact and effectiveness. A powerful intention coalesces one's thinking, belief and emotions around the transformation one wants to create. Intention focuses the direction of one's efforts and helps chart the way forward. Intention is a deeply subjective mindset arising out of a personal life story, which becomes a platform for change and transformation. Impact and effectiveness, however, happen in the application of one's intention on others moving them to do creative things. Effectiveness happens in the external theatre where one's personal life story engages effectively with the reality of the situation. Great achievers make things happen in developing the world as their ideas, intentions resonate with significant others. All of us have potential for being great achievers provided we are prepared to do the right things. There is need to focus on five essential skills.

The first skill is the ability to focus on causes and effects of the volatile, uncertain, complex and ambiguous world. Dubey (2012) suggests that one needs to make sense of the VUCA world. A good achiever should have the ability to create a long term vision and deep expertise in some specific domain. This involves the ability to move through the overload of information which clutters the present day brave VUCA world. One should be able to identify focus areas and then get deep into the flow of transformational innovation.

The second skill is the ability to use the whole mind in any situation where the left brain of logic, reason and rationality is combined with the right brain of intuition, empathy, connection and innovation.

The third skill is the ability to work harmoniously with others towards a common goal. One should be a multiplier of energy, passion, engagement and ownership of a project. This involves a shift from a command and control mindset to listening, collaborating, encouraging, asking the right questions and co-creating answers, as well as solutions to problems. Here the emphasis is on following up a passion that would result in success following the passion.

The fourth skill is the ability to make space for calculated risk and innovation. One should be able to encourage innovation by creating a culture where people can dare to take risks for creativity and invention.

The fifth skill resides in the ability to create a socio culture of trust, honesty and walk the talk. This skill requires the ability to remove the mask and be who one is. Thinking, saying and doing are totally aligned.

Summation

We have strived, in this chapter, to show the importance of causes of economic growth, the place of investment portfolios, prudent entrepreneurs, smart and enterprising persons within and across countries. These are the people who make things happen while some watch things happen and others wonder what has happened. The place and role of prudent investment of resources, time, effort, energy and mind ensures that individuals and nations become, and remain rich, comfortable and afloat while others sink into poverty. The power is in our hands as individuals, groups and nations. The socio economic world belongs to those who are hard working, diligent, scrupulous, daring, enterprising, and investment driven. The more we train and educate people to work on resource enterprise, the higher the level and standard of living the people would enjoy. This, among other efforts, makes a difference between prosperity and poverty. People cannot be developed, they can only develop themselves.

For Reflection

Suggest three strategies a person needs to cope with the VUCA world we live in? What should one invest in the context of an under developed country?

Justify what you consider to be a safe investment.

Barriers to Growth and Development

In chapter 5 we have examined the causes of economic growth. We saw how properly planned, and designed programmes serve as vital ingredients, and not inhibitors, to economic growth, and how markets and fiscal discipline can help promote growth, development, education and social justice.

In this chapter we analyse barriers to growth and development at the individual, group and national levels. Some of the barriers cross borders to affect international and world levels. As we have seen, economic growth requires that, among other things, countries use their available resources more efficiently and add value to their products. If the resource base is limited it becomes an obstacle to growth and development. Barriers to growth and development stem from micro and macro economic causes.

The Causes and effects of inflation

This area of socio economics has given rise to one of the most significant macro economic headaches in all nations. There are basically two causes of inflation. Demand pull inflation is brought about by an increase in demand for a good or service. There are essentially two divergent points of view on factors that lead to inflation. The monetarists argue that inflation is brought about by the amount of money in the economy. In other words the spending power of the populace exceeds the capacity of the country to produce goods and services. They also argue that government over spending leads to budget deficits which fuel inflation. High levels of government spending on supporting a large bureaucratic civil service and bailing out inefficient parastatals contribute to inflation. Printing of more money, or borrowing, both increases the amount of money supply in the system. All this leads to too much money chasing too few goods. So to the monetarists, the solution is to control money supply through austerity measures such as realistic employment levels, realistic wages and prices.

Non monetarists argue that spending is not only dependent on the amount of money in the system but also on how rapidly it is used. This velocity of circulation varies and adjusts leading to the economy over heating. The amount of money in the economy responds to changes in the price levels. (Keith and Gubellini, 1980).

The other cause of inflation is cost push inflation which is caused by increases in the cost factors of production such as raw materials, fuel, energy, wages and water. These are also referred to as fuels of inflation. So producers have to pass on the cost to the consumer. Other factors that fuel inflation are increases in wage settlements not related to productivity levels. Devaluation or depreciation of currency can lead to increases in prices of both local and imported goods and services. Direct and indirect tax and levies in the economy can lead to inflationary pressures on the economy.

Problems associated with high rates of inflation are many. Rising prices cause worsening poverty as the essentials for survival become more expensive and out of reach of ordinary people. Family incomes lose their power to pay for basic commodities, decent accommodation, basic education and health care. Ever rising prices cause anxiety and uncertainty at the individual, group and societal levels. In such a situation it is difficult for people to make savings. Without savings there is no investment. Without investment, the economy stagnates, leading to under employment and unemployment.

Capital Resources

Shortages in capital resources are linked to barriers to growth and development. Inadequate amounts and levels of capital goods and finance, especially in developing countries, can lead to retarded growth and development. Internal formation occurs through savings leading to investment. Lack of savings may mean lack of investment in real and human capital. Capital flight to safer destinations abroad reduces the number of investors and entrepreneurs to stimulate the economy. All this may lead to poor infrastructure, low GDP, backward technologies, under employment and poverty.

Institutional Factors

Institutional factors relate to internal, international and global restrictive policies and practices. Social, cultural, religious and ethnic beliefs can create either a favourable or unfavourable environment for achieving economic growth. Social events and activities such as ethnic, gender, religious and racial preferences lead to institutional inefficiency. Political institutions can enhance, or hinder growth and development. Good governance enshrining: fair play, social justice, honesty, productivity, self correcting mechanisms, rule of law, equality and transparency create a good environment for investment, production and growth. On the other hand political institutions that foster corruption, intolerance, waste, poor and selective law enforcement, human rights violations, narrow individual and sectarian interests and agendas… are severe impediments to growth and development.

Technological Institutions

Technological advances correlate positively with levels of economic production and high standards of living. Investment, savings in labour, time and effort are engines of productivity leading to socio economic development. Out dated, obsolete and primitive technologies are cost-inefficient, unreliable and less effective. For a country to experience sustained economic growth it should have better technology, advanced human resources, and more efficient management of natural resources. Abundance of natural resources in a country, in itself, does not necessarily lead to socio economic development. Many developing countries are endowed with natural resources but they remain in poverty and human strife. The Democratic Republic of Congo is the most endowed country, in natural resources, in the world. Almost all the natural resources are found there. But it is the most troubled country in the world. It could be because the resources fall into the wrong foreign hands that foster strife so as to benefit from the rich natural resources. The Africans cry the beloved country. By contrast, Japan has poor natural resources, yet it has developed its human, technological and institutional resources to add value to other people's resources to great advantage.

Human Resources

Developing countries experience wastes in human resources through unemployment, under employment, migration and over population. The countries end up with unskilled personnel especially in critical areas. So the economies find it difficult to develop human capital resources. Education and training of human resources is left to less capable people lacking in skills, knowledge, professionalism and motivation. The exodus of the best and brightest academic and professional minds, leave behind vacuums to be filled up by often incompetent, inexperienced people lacking in sophistication. Growing populations reduce the countries' capacity to save, invest and increase productivity. The populace tend to over use, abuse and plunder land and natural resources, ending up living in squalid conditions in urban areas. All this leads to vicious cycles of poverty. In itself, a high population is not a cause of poverty. It is the quality of the populace in terms of enterprise, levels of sophistication and education that lead to economic growth. Good examples are Japan, Great Britain, Germany and Hong Kong.

International and Global Barriers

A country's problems of development are linked to the level of debts, borrowings and reliance on externally driven market forces. International trade tariffs and quotas weigh heavily against countries that depend on exports of primary products from agriculture and mining. They do not control the prices of their primary commodities. Instead they have to re import goods made from their own primary products. They lack the capacity to add value to the primary products before exporting to other countries. Because they cannot balance their economic books they rely on borrowings from the developed world. Strings attached to the debts lead to further problems of repayment, structural adjustment programmes and restrictions. A typical example is that of African oil producing countries. They export to Europe and America crude oil at cheap prices, only to import back oil refined products at higher prices. For relief, and balance of payments, they have to borrow from the World Bank through its sister organisation the International Monetary Fund.

Poverty and the Cycles of Poverty

Poverty can be considered in absolute and relative terms. Absolute poverty is where the level of income is below the minimum requirements for survival, such as food, health care, shelter and schooling. However, relative poverty relates to the standard of living falling below a certain percentage of a country's average.

Poverty affects economic growth in many ways. Low income earners spend most of their income on consumables. As incomes are low, savings are also low since they live from hand to mouth. Hence, the availability of funds for domestic and internal investment is thus limited. Poverty also means that capital, productivity and motivation suffer. Since income is invariably linked to productivity financial returns diminish. Because poor people cannot afford health care, decent shelter and basic education, it follows that their children suffer the same fate. They cannot break the poverty trap. Both these cycles feed into each other, and once in the trap, the momentum is self perpetuating. The poverty cycle is complete. Once that happens it is very difficult to lift oneself out of absolute poverty.

Strategies for Poverty Eradication

The critical areas in poverty alleviation and eradication revolve on priorities such as: increasing levels of productivity, incomes, savings, investment, education and health provision. The debate is on ways in which all this should be done.

The first strategy was the development of assistance philosophy, which argued that poor countries suffered from deficiency of finance, skills, knowledge and motivation to produce, plan, think, save and invest. So direct injection of aid would kick start economic growth. Outsider driven programmes were designed, planned and implemented with large to medium scale of inputs from governments, the World Bank and donor groups. It was believed that government and big business spending would trickle down to those poor people of the targeted country. However, though there was economic growth, levels of absolute poverty continued, and even worsened.

The second strategy was put in place that aimed at the basic human needs of the poor people in the targeted countries. Rich countries of the world poured in money through aid agencies, donor groups and the World Bank. Integrated Rural programmes providing access to safe water, basic education and primary health care were embarked on. Still absolute poverty stubbornly remained. Reasons like failure by external driven efforts failed to involve the social institutions and basic infrastructure of the communities. Projects collapsed as soon as the donor left. There was no ownership of the projects. There was also discontent concerning many aid organisations with their self serving bureaucracies.

The third strategy was aimed at reducing country deficits by making markets poor country friendly through tariff concessions, preferential treatment of poor country goods into European markets. Examples were the Lome Convention with its special concessions on tariffs and prices. Official development assistance focused on market solutions and liberalisation of the economy to stimulate growth. Still poverty stubbornly refused to go.

A fourth strategy was increased aid for market related programmes based on the poor people themselves getting directly involved in the identification, planning, designing and implementing their own development projects. This is an insider driven development strategy where the programmes are based on felt needs of groups as beneficiaries. Micro finance schemes for capital inputs are put in place supported by aid agencies. At the macro level trade for developing countries should concentrate on finished products rather than primary products. The global market should favour poor countries' finished products. There is evidence that these latter strategies are helping in alleviating problems in primary health care, basic education, basic infrastructure, as well as combating endemic diseases such as HIV/Aids and malaria.

Arguments against Foreign Aid

Evidence is emerging that as aid to Africa has grown, the continent has become poorer rather than better off. Poverty, hunger, disease, strife and suffering prevail. This is a paradox of development. So there are calls for a paradigm shift towards self generated and self driven strategies to make the poor come out of their poverty. At the end of the 2nd world war the most destroyed nations of the world, Germany and Japan, lifted themselves by their torn boot straps to become the world's economic giants, in a space of under 50 years. Given ideas, motivation, determination and enterprise the poor people of the world can rise and shine economically. The Japanese have improved on the Chinese rod and fish philosophy that if persons ask for fish show them how to grow and farm fish. People are poor because they do not want to think. It is the result of poverty of mind and expecting to be given hand outs. The dependency syndrome will continue feeding into the vicious cycles of poverty.

Right wing groups in the west argue that foreign aid creates a number of problems. Aid often falls into the hands of corrupt officials affecting the development projects. Location of the projects usually go to the officials' own privileged areas, not poor ones. Aid money is often misspent or diverted to non essential projects like sports stadiums, luxury hotels, cars and aircraft. Worse, the funds can be spent on arms to repress the very poor people and keep them in their place. The social costs of aid can be catastrophic to the very poor people.

Other pressure groups in the west also complain that aid can give the impression among receiving countries that giving countries are wealthy, free handed donors with infinite sources. Aid also gives a false sense of security, and that those receiving it, have a right to aid. Aid also encourages many people in recipient countries to migrate to the source of wealth with hopes of finding prosperity.

Dependency theory debases the motive for aid as a patronising act of charity. Recipient countries find it difficult to oppose the views, though wrong, of aid giving countries especially at public forums.

Obscurantismo

For obscurantismo refer to Machel's theory of economic growth and development, and the glossary. Obscurantismo is viewed as a very serious barrier to growth and development especially in Africa and less developed countries.

False economy

False economy is a serious barrier to economic growth and development. It was long explained by Karl Marx as the false impression one has of thinking that one is benefiting from an economic system when in fact it is paltry and desultory. Workers would think they are benefiting when they are given monkey nuts as salary and wages. The beneficiary would be the capitalist, the owner of the means, forces and fruits of production. The practice of false economy has been with the world for a long time.

The ancient Egyptian sage would give the story of a wolf fallen into a deep well and could not come out by its own efforts. When a goat with young ones inquired what the wolf was doing in the deep well, the wolf said it was enjoying the sweet water down there. It invited the goat down the deep well. After some hesitation the goat went down the well. The wolf stamped on the back of the goat and leapt from the deep well. Having escaped from the deep well the wolf drove the young goats promising to keep them safe from predators. At a safe distant cave from the well the wolf took one male goat for a walk and ate it. Other goats were kept in the dark as they started breeding. The wolf continued to protect the goats as it had a ready source of meat. The story is relevant to people of the present time.

In this world, many leap out and rise up in life by mercilessly stamping on others and leaving them to miserable plights. Others are often made scapegoats. Most winnings are the results of the defeat of others. Win-lose game rules say you cannot win unless others lose. You cannot be at the top unless you keep everyone else under you. This is why leaders want to remain on top of others. This is why we feel threatened by the presence of capable people.

In terms of economic growth and development no one is charitable. Life is full of overt and covert motives. People want excessive profits, gains and advantages. Who controls world trade, international markets and products? A country exports a barrel of oil, the receiving country refines the crude oil into 12 products and makes a thousand per cent profit. A country sells gold, diamonds, platinum...the international buyer makes two thousand per cent profit. A country sells cocoa and the buyer makes a killing in profit and products. Farmers in a developing country sell tobacco to an international buyer who makes a fortune from leaf and stem used in the manufacture of bullets and armaments. Poor people in Africa sell cellular air time for peanuts, who gets most of the money? Some persons bank their money with offshore banks, who uses the money for investment the person or bank owners? False economy makes people, especially in Africa poor, debt ridden and under developed.

Possible Solutions to Development Challenges

Solutions to development challenges have been discussed as each aspect was covered. Most solutions depend on individual view points, circumstances, locality and preferred modus operandi. All the same it is useful to look at general possible solutions especially for developing countries in Africa.

Role of Individuals and Groups in Socio economic Growth

It is imperative that people should be educated and empowered to work on their own problems and proffer solutions. For problems are solutions in disguise. Humans spring into action under a sting than a caress. Projects should emanate from individual and group felt needs. It is those directly affected who feel where the shoe pinches, where the thorn hurts in the foot. People should be taught to be self starting, bold, self motivating and enterprising. Education curricula should teach people to solve problems, to create, to invent, to think and analyse issues and situations.

At the individual and group level economic projects based on needs, interests, situation and circumstances can be ventured into with little capital resources. These should be able to supplement one's main source of income. Streams of income are essential if one is to increase the income base. Project identification is critical. One could start on projects that meet one's immediate needs like clothes, shoes, pieces of furniture, detergents, natural cosmetics, fruit, vegetables, flowers, meat, eggs and herbs. Surpluses can then be sold to friends, relatives and neighbours.

Pole of Growth Model

A pole of growth is a socio economic growth and development model that views human development in carefully planned stages that lead to self sufficiency. It is an integrated model which emphasises that individuals, groups and nations should have a central point around which growth and development spring from. The foci radiate basic needs, goals, means, inputs, through puts and outputs, as resources permit. The model is as old as humanity. Civilisations evolved around poles of growth. The Egyptian civilisation grew on the Nile river, Babylonian citadel on the Tigris and Euphrates, Roman empire on the river Tiber, Great Zimbabwe on the Mutirikwi river, the British empire on the river Thames. From the pole of growth, larger segments can be added to add value to the model.

Project planning involves capital resources, marketing patterns and processes, scope and potential for expansion. With time, effort, experience and more resources these could develop into more serious projects deserving to be called centres or poles of growth. These can start off as hobbies to become serious income generating projects. More land, capital, equipment, machinery, structures can be acquired as the pole of growth develops. Many a big enterprise started as a hobby. These can be started in one's back yard, in town, service centre or rural area. All locations on earth, and in space, have windows of opportunity for starting viable income generating projects.

Micro Projects

Micro projects can be started in the service sector in one's place of residence, at first to avoid crippling side costs such as rent, cost of energy and water. Examples of mini income generating projects are small remedial teaching groups, guidance and counselling sessions, information technology instruction, herb and cosmetics making lessons, play centres for children, organising old people tours to local interesting places, bee keeping programmes using local resources, athletics and sport coaching clinics, shrub/flower/fruit/vegetable seedling nurseries.

The rule of thumb is that once a project has taken off, is bringing in good income on a sustained basis, the project owner should put in full time attention if it is to grow into a bigger project. The owner should have the courage to go into it on a full time basis. Many a country's industry has started as individual and group driven micro projects needing inexpensive resources to begin with. Streams of income from such small ventures lead to savings that lead to investment in bigger ventures. This approach could be one of the most effective ways of generating employment, income, savings, investment, and ultimately eradicating poverty.

The Place of Self employment in Socio economic Growth and Development

Many people wish to be self employed but for a variety of reasons have not made the move. Reasons range from fear of failure and the unknown, inertia, perceived insecurity, age either too young or too old, to lack of funds and guts.

A small number, who venture into self employment, give a variety of reasons. Some feel that they need to be independent from patronising authority. They would rather have the ultimate authority of the customer. Some want to be completely responsible for their own growth and development, socially, economically and passionately. Some would want to maintain a family tradition in continuing with what the fore-bearers were involved in. While others sought to maximise earnings, get maximum profits and be rich. Wealth would give them comfort in life, working or retired. They site many professionals, academics, politicians and sports persons who have ended up destitute, especially in the evening of their lives.

In short, the move to self employment depends on factors such as personal desire, achievement motivation, courage and the means to start the socio economic venture. What ever the reasons they give for going into self employment, most of them eventually succeed. In the process they contribute significantly to their own, and the nation's, socio economic growth and development. Many big corporations are either individually, or family owned. Examples are: Anglo American Corporation, De Beers, Coca Cola, Bata International, the Walton family (Wal-Mart), the Hunt family (the Texas Oil firm), the Ford family, and Toyoda family (Toyota corporation).

The Bio-economy Strategy

The bio-economy strategy is the use of bio-scientific knowledge, research, development and innovation so as to enhance employment creation, food security, good health and sustainable development. The strategy utilises indigenous knowledge systems involving local biodiversity of fauna and flora. Systematic research and development should unlock the value of indigenous resources such as their curative, nutritional and palliative properties. Africa's indigenous fauna and flora, coupled with the world consumer demand for natural products, presents opportunities for Africa to capitalise on its bio-diversity and capture a lucrative niche in the economic market. Flora that have great potential are indigenous plants like the moringa tree, the African potato, natural sweetener monatin, rooibos tea, honey-bush, marijuana, fortified sorghum, protea and African lily flowers, and the bamboo.

The bamboo plant is one of the indigenous plants that can create tremendous opportunities for micro and macro-economic projects. It can be made into robust, lasting and beautiful furniture, flooring material, baskets, curtains, stain resisting artefacts and many luxurious articles. All these have local, regional and international markets. Bamboo is the fastest growing woody plant on earth, and can grow in the tropical and equatorial regions of the world, especially in Africa. It offers 25 times the yield of hardwood. It is harder than red oak and North American maple. It needs no sawing, planing and painting. Bamboo can be harvested without killing the plant. It is such a hardy plant that it requires no pesticides or fertilizers. It can grow 1.5 metres a month, making it the greenest, cleanest environmental plants on planet earth.

Africa's fauna are legendary in terms of economic and gastronomic excellence. Even the little quails' eggs, besides looking pretty on display, have become established as one of the world's contemporary cook's ingredients. The raw eggs are effective medicinal remedies for disease and ailments. Quails can be easily, and cheaply, raised for local and export markets.

To realise the potential of this bio-diversity there is urgent need for interventionist strategies. First there should be local and regional coordinating committees consisting of experts in different areas. The committees should prioritise resource allocation, guide implementation plans, coordinate research and monitor progress, and recommend initiatives.

Second, there should be bio-economy innovation hubs. The knowledge, skills and solutions emerging from bio-technology research and development should be effectively transferred to small scale and commercial enterprises. Local and regional innovation hubs should act as catalysts for producing, processing, distributing and marketing by the innovators. The role of indigenous knowledge systems are critical in enhancing local and grassroots innovation, discovery and improving of the quality and quantity of life. This area has the potential to develop key skills in managing plant breeding, agronomics, biometry, bio-control, and bio fertigation.

Third, bio-diverse resource processing initiatives help add value to primary products, reduce post harvest losses, extend shelf life, and improve the quality and safety of finished products.

Fourth, energy initiatives involving renewable energy sources such as solar, hydro, wind and bio-fuels have great potential for research, development and practical applications for Africa and the world.

Fifth, a critical area that needs attention for bio-economy initiatives to succeed is funding. Co-funding strategies should be put in place. Research, development, centres and processing plants need money. So co-funding initiatives involving, ordinary citizens, donors, commerce, industry, government and civic organisations can garner considerable resources to fund the bio-economy strategy.

The Role of Government

Governments should create enabling environments for economic growth and development. Benevolent politics, sound policies and prudent practices should be put in place to foster individual, group and company investment. Tax regimes should encourage economic growth. People oriented policies and practices should stimulate economic progress. Socio economic issues should drive politics not the other way round. The populace should put political power in the hands of people who are capable of nurturing economic growth and development. Candidates for political posts must have track records in initiating successful development projects. People of merit, integrity and substance should occupy political office.

Governments should also enshrine the principles of rule of law, capital formation, social justice, equality, freedom of speech and choice, and transparency. Other socio economic priorities should ensure opening economies to international trade, building human capital, making peace with neighbours, privatising state enterprises and holding free and fair elections on time.

Role of Industrially Advanced Countries

Industrially advanced countries have to play their part in funding macro projects especially in areas of energy development, rail, road, and port infrastructure development. They should lower trade barriers by removing tariffs and quotas on products and goods from developing countries. They should discourage brain drains of skilled personnel from less developed nations. They must stop the sale of weapons and arms to developing countries. Davidson (1994).

Rules of Thumb for Starting a Socio economic Project

The days of working at a job for a life time in the hope of relying on a pension are long gone. A job is a form of equity. No job is safe and secure. A job can be affected by a number of problems. It can end abruptly. The employer can go bankrupt. Even governments, parastatals and big business can go broke. Salaries and wages can seriously decline due to poor remuneration, poor income, depreciation in currencies, mismanagement and misappropriation of resources. So one needs to move towards self sufficiency, self empowerment, comfort and, even richness.

The following rules of thumb are essential towards success in a socio economic project at the micro level, to begin with.

1. Overcome fear. Fear stands for False Evidence Appearing Real. Fear of the unknown makes people inert. One should develop a fighter's attitude, that is, to overcome fear of failure, of making mistakes, of criticism and of rejection.

2. Be proactive by focusing on a want for a particular project. One should decide on a project based on interest and passion. One should be oneself and original. Avoid aping what others are doing. Have a project that is aligned with who one is, norms and values.

3. Work by design and frames of mind. One has to know what one wants to do, the knowledge, experiences and skills needed. The enthusiasm, interest, motivation and ambitions should clearly be formulated.

4. Set achievable goals, aims and objectives. These will make the project succeed. There is need to balance economic, environmental, social, moral and ethical norms. The name, logo and motto should say it all.

5. Planning is critical. One should always set up project on own property where one has title deeds to oneself. Rely on own resources as much as possible. Avoid borrowing and debts. Save for it. A critical part of planning includes succession planning. Business project success should make it from first, second, third and fourth generation. There should be continuity and improvement of the business project. Active participation by young members of the immediate family should be done even with grand children. A willing and able cohort of successors should be identified and empowered with skills, knowledge, finance, time frames, goals and motivation. When the business is quite established it should be legally and professionally structured as a trust to avoid wrangles, transfer of ownership and re sales.

6. Start small and aim to become big eventually. Partners should be very limited. Immediate, close family members are best at starting a project. Normally family members have same levels of interest, motivation and needs. Many successful businesses in the world started as family projects.

7. Move towards being an expert in the project. There is need to learn, know and practise the skills, knowledge and innuendos regarding the project. This would enhance turnover, profit and popularity.

8. Have real value that benefits people, fauna and flora. The community, country, region and the world should benefit from a good, sound and vibrant project.

9. Execution is the way to go with a project. Talk and spreading ideas do not make the project take off. The project has to be started and worked on.

10. Do not give up; network with significant others. Most successful socio economic projects would have reached difficult stages but determination, hard work, learning from significant others made them pull through. Project development has its birth pains, growing challenges and difficulties that need to be overcome. Perseverance, resilience and finding innovative ways around challenges set winners apart.

If a project is well designed, planned and executed it should succeed. The project owner, developer should follow the motto 'There is a way', and will make a way round all adversity like a champion. Success in socio economic projects comes if they are aligned to the owner's passion, interest, goals, belief of what the world needs.

For Reflection

Discuss the place of bio-diversity in socio economic growth and development. Design, and justify, a micro project with potential for growing into a macro enterprise.

Analyse the assertion that Africa's unemployment solution lies in self reliant projects.

The Political Causes of Poverty: Agrarian Reform vis-a-vis Socio economic and Development Challenges

Abstract

It is the argument of this case study that development cannot take root in a situation where agrarian reform is illogical, haphazard and directionless. In the process of such a scenario socio economic growth and education suffer in many irreparable ways. Instead of addressing inequality and poverty among marginalized groups, it sharpens and deepens inequality and poverty. To alleviate the plight of vulnerable groups radical and fair action is needed. The Zimbabwean land crusades were not agrarian reform because they lack essential elements of a national program. For it to become agrarian reform, the program should have a comprehensive policy, a regulative policy, institutional development, capacity building, a systematic transparent land registration plan, civic and human rights respects, ; civil participation, self development capacity for land management and sustainable development. . Above all it should be based on ethical, non racial, moral and international legal considerations. . Basic human rights must not be sacrificed on the altar of political expedient attempts to correct past, and perceived, inequalities. Because of the irrational, chaotic and haphazard land reform program, the country descended into abject poverty, hunger and suffering. It did not lead to fair and equal access to land by the majority of the population.

Operating Terms

Agrarian reform, access to productive land, and land tenure are critical and closely interlinked. They invariably affect socio economic, health, educational and social service indicators. Agrarian reform implies a planned development land program under pinned by a comprehensive land policy and regulatory framework. Access to productive land implies fair distribution, sustained utilization and development of land. Land tenure on the other hand implies property user rights of soil, water, fauna and flora resources, based on a national systematic, lawful land registration program.

History of Land Tenure Systems

In all countries land tenure systems have a long history, reflecting political, socio economic and educational development. During periods of socio political transition the restoration of past land rights enters into conflict with existing land laws and user rights. In Southern Africa in general, and Namibia, South Africa and Zimbabwe in particular, the restoration of past land rights of formerly marginalized African population groups became contentious issues after the fall of the colonial regimes. The restoration of traditional rights to land may need economic, political and social will to guarantee and protect these rights. But there are other land rights that actually belong to the first land occupiers, such as the San (Bushmen), Congoids, Khoikoi (Hottentots). They occupied East and Southern Africa, long before the Bantu who constitute the majority of the present African population in East and Southern Africa. So the restoration of land rights helps to balance socio economic imbalances and injustices. But if not handled carefully it may create new injustices, moral and ethical dilemmas. It can cause massive socio economic, political and educational damage to the affected country, and even its neighbours in the region.

Struggles over control and ownership of land continue to be a feature of contemporary political conflicts in different parts of the world. Land reform has become a human rights obligation and a policy measure for social justice and economic development. Furthermore, land redistribution is regarded as a panacea to landlessness, land concentration, poverty reduction and hunger. (IFAD, 2001). Around the world the poorest of the poor are the landless in rural and urban areas. The next in line of the poorest are those whose poor quality pieces of land cannot support a family. Studies of the outcome of virtually all land reform programs, carried out in low income countries in the world, show that land distribution is a very effective way to foster development, and improve people's welfare. (Diouf, 2004).

Counter Arguments to Land Redistribution

However, there are counter arguments to land redistribution. The first and fundamental questions to be addressed and answered are: Who is indigenous in Central, East and Southern Africa? Who were the first people to occupy land? Are they the Congoids, Khoikoi, San, early Bantu people, or the late Bantu groups? Who has the right of title to land? To which human group should land be redistributed and why? Is the right of power and conquest the legal basis to title on land? How far back in history on land should we go? Even as late as July 2005, the San in Botswana were suffering eviction from their traditional land in the arid region. The Botswana authorities claim that the San should be moved from their land, ostensibly to protect the land from poaching activities; and to give the San a more secure sedentary life style with education, health, electricity and water services. But the real motive could be the desire to exploit the rich mineral resources in the traditional land of the San. It has happened several times before. In colonial Rhodesia the indigenous Tonga people of the Zambezi valley were evicted from their traditional land to make way for the construction of the Kariba Dam. Up to now, the Tonga have not benefitted from the hydro electricity or, water from the Kariba dam.

The second argument against land redistribution is based on inert human nature. Agrarian reform often leads to conflict of interest because it involves redistribution of property. True to Karl Marx's theory of resistance to change, those with productive land resources seldom offer enough land on a voluntary basis. So agrarian reform often requires expropriation measures and what is considered fair compensation. The economically powerful landowners invest heavily in agro-industrial enterprises producing surpluses for home and export markets. The economically powerful entrepreneurial people achieve local, national, regional and global food security because of their modern, intensive and sophisticated production processes. They provide cheap affordable products, employment and other facilities. Redistributing the highly productive land to poor people can be counter-productive leading to economic and development melt down. Politicians tend to favour such land redistribution to gain political mileage, but for short term gains. Poverty grows fast as the situation deteriorates.

The third argument belongs to the political economy of the conflict paradigm. Conflict is polarized around the greed versus grievance dichotomy that normally translates into, at best, justice seeking, and at worst, loot seeking strategies. Combatant self enrichment motives and opportunities for insurgent mobilization surface under weak, unregulated, undemocratic, unaccountable governments, and state failure. Ballentine and Nitzschke, (2003) posit that such weak, corrupt governance creates situations where opportunistic groups and individuals access lootable resources such as alluvial gold, diamonds, narcotics, coltan, wildlife products, moveable property and equipment. These looting activities interact to varying degrees with long standing socio economic and political grievances, inter ethnic disputes over land and resources, security and legal dilemmas. So policies for conflict management need to be based on comprehensive approaches that take into account governance, legal, ethical, socio economic, political and educational dynamics. So findings from the conflict paradigm, and lessons for policy, call for local, and international resource control regimes that help control conflict, be it land, or other natural resources. So a legal, rational, moral, ethical and civilized approach to the issue of land is necessary to avoid doing more harm to the very marginalized people needing improving their lives. UNCTAD (2003) reports that even in countries that have redistributed land rather fairly well, poverty is growing fast as the situation of the poor is deteriorating.

The Zimbabwean Experience

Zimbabwe gained independence in 1980 after a bitter and protracted liberation war. Out of the 12 million inhabitants, 5000 white commercial farmers owned 45% of the country's productive land. Rich whites such as the South African Oppenheimer family owned estates as large as 2.4 million acres, equal to half the size of Belgium. The Lancaster House Agreement of 1979, that ushered in independence, limited the land reform process for 10 years. So the white commercial farmers, who acquired the land titles for the past 100 years, continued to use the best land of the country. They continued to produce huge surpluses for home and export markets, making Zimbabwe the food basket of Africa. The African communities remained mainly with marginal land, but benefitted in many ways from agro based industrial and commercial production.

Land utilization in the African occupied areas suffered a number of set-backs. Increasing population put a lot of pressure on the traditional land tenure system. Poor land management practices contributed to severe land and water resource degradation. Resettlement schemes, well funded by donors, failed to increase productivity for reasons like corruption, lack of knowledge and relevant skills, insufficient financial, institutional and technical support. Increasing poverty, lack of government sensitivity to the plight of the landless, the unwillingness of white farmers to share their surplus land exaggerated the situation. All this resulted in high pressure for land, and unpopularity of an ineffective government. Although socio political pressure for land reform increased, the government had no concept as it remained inactive. It only meekly blamed the British and white farmers. Some vacant land was given to some influential ruling party individuals.

But much later, due to fears of losing political power, the ruling party took the land reform issue on agenda. They belatedly called for land occupation through the activities of party militants calling themselves liberation war veterans. These, in fact, were young squatters from urban centres to be protected and overseen by police, security agents and some soldiers. The argument put forward was that old colonial land laws and land titles were no longer valid. But the argument ignored the fact that the post colonial African government had given title deeds, and registered 80% of the farms held by the white commercial farmers. That means that 80% of the white farmers had actually bought and paid for their land after independence with the permission and consent of the Zimbabwean government; particularly those who registered their title deeds only after a certificate of no interest from government was issued as required since 1986.

The Agrarian Reform Went Awry

In the year 2000, Robert Gabriel Mugabe's government embarked on a racial, chaotic and controversial land redistribution program. Most white commercial farmers lost their land in a space of six months. The operation was accompanied by violence, looting, crime and lawlessness. Its fall out was the displacement, mainly of African workers, a substantial number of whom came from neighbouring countries such as Malawi and Mozambique. The whites, the black workers, children and families lost their employment, sources of their livelihood, food, shelter, education and social security. The government promoted the violent take-over of white owned farms as a futile way of regaining African popular support, and rewarding political allies.

On the other hand the new occupiers of the land lacked skills, motivation, knowledge and resources. Not only did productivity fall but law and order deteriorated.

Reports from Amnesty International (2002) said the land occupations led to unprecedented violence, forced removal of thousands of white farmers, their workers and dependents, from the farms. Displaced farm workers and their children lost shelter, employment, schools and health facilities. In typical political economy terms justice seeking became loot seeking driven by greed versus grievance dichotomy. Farm infrastructure was destroyed, equipment and machinery looted. Farm production fell drastically, environmental degradation increased; and the whole economy, which was mainly agro based, collapsed. The socio economic fallout eclipsed even that of countries at war: Amnesty International concluded.

A Zimbabwe government land audit (2004) said that, regrettably most of the seized farms fell into the hands of the ruling party heavy weights, not in the hands of poor landless people. The land audit reported wide spread cases of senior party authorities having grabbed more than one farm for themselves. In many cases ordinary people were evicted, by the big guns, from the farms they had occupied to make way for the political heavy weights. At worst, the political heavy weights looted, moving from one farm to the next at whim. The rural areas remain congested as before, with their poor degraded land resources.

Transparency International (2006) reported that the Zimbabwean land seizures have led to a no win situation for the country. Only 400 white farmers out of the original 5000 farmers were still operational. Over 200 000 black farm workers lost employment, shelter and food leading to destitution and grinding poverty. Their children lost school and health facilities. Almost all of the former farm workers, many of whom have very good farming skills and knowledge, had no access to the occupied land. On the other hand the new farm occupiers have no farming experience, no knowledge, no capital, no infrastructure, no equipment... hence no will and motivation to work on the land. Urban areas lost food and agro based products for commerce and industry. The country lost its main source of foreign exchange earnings and trade, leading to acute shortages of fuel, spare parts, medicines, and other essential commodities. The chaos on the farms had cost the country US$500 billion. Wongibe (2005) noted that for the Zimbabwe government, the land occupations were socio economic and political kamikaze, hara-kiri and suicide from which they could not resurrect. A crippled economy, a state of perpetual lawlessness, hunger...and a nation increasingly isolated by the rest of the world, is all the Zimbabwe government has to show for its land policies.

As we write in 2015, close to 8 million Zimbabweans are in need of emergency food aid because of the impact of the land occupations, and to some extent the drought that has hit Southern Africa. The country has to import food from countries like Zambia and Mozambique that depend on farming from former Zimbabwean white farmers who were removed from Zimbabwe.

Summary of an Unprecedented Crisis

A genuine land issue went wildly awry because it was belated, haphazard, opportunistic, unplanned and ruthless. Zimbabwe faces economic, social, political and humanitarian crises. Poor economic policies become bad politics. The economy is almost dead. The economic crisis is characterised by acute shortages of foreign currency, fuel, electricity, essential commodities, food, drugs, essential chemicals, educational materials, money for saving and investment, and even blood for transfusion. The local currency has become so worthless that the country now relies on imported basket of foreign currency such as US dollar, British pound, Euro currency. The social crisis manifests itself in unprecedented unemployment reaching 90%, the collapse of the health delivery system; unstable and deteriorating education system. The GDP has dropped to US$350 with over 80% of the population living on less than US$2 a day. Game reserves have been reduced to waste lands through poaching and invasion by highly placed individuals, in government, police, secret service and army.

The socio economic, educational, political and humanitarian crises affected the whole of the Southern Region. The crises have drawn in the African Union, SAADIC, the Commonwealth of Nations, the European Union and the United Nations. Almost all of it, because of a misguided, haphazard, narrow minded and un-planned agrarian reform program. The social, political, economic and educational crises now facing the country date from the government sponsored invasion of white owned land. This destroyed agricultural production, vital exports. It frightened away direct investment, and helped make the country an international pariah. This was the genesis of the country's socio economic woes, since 75% of the country's income came from agricultural exports. Most of the grabbed farms lie idle, over grown with weeds, and trees indiscriminately cut down. The countryside look blighted by a terrible scourge, and half the population depend on food aid. Many more subsist on roots, and fried termites as they are reduced to destitution. The country that was the region's food basket has become a basket case.

Nevertheless, the underlying principles of equitable redistribution of land resources remain in spite of the serious mistakes made to implement it. So, great lessons can be learnt from the Zimbabwean experience.

For South Africa and Namibia

In South Africa and Namibia land ownership patterns are very similar to the then Zimbabwean scenario. South Africa is dealing with a deeply entrenched racially dominated land tenure system. IFAD (2001) reports that small holders, mainly African, in South Africa control less than13% of the agricultural land, while 87% belongs to 60 000 white commercial farmers. And these commercial farmers produce state of the art agro industrial and commercial products for home and export markets. In Namibia, 5 000 white commercial farmers own 80% of the land while 20% belongs to African small land holders.

The best advice for potential African commercial farmers in the two countries is to understudy quietly the techniques used by the white experienced farmers. Apprenticeship schemes should be made to enhance Africans in commercial and agro based farm production.

For the moment the two countries have prudently opted for the World Bank and IMF concept of 'willing seller, willing buyer' market oriented land acquisition formula, for land redistribution, with the government providing the funding. This has apparently procured South Africa and Namibia a stable and lawful environment which is conducive, meaningful sustained development. But the formula has led to slow paces in acquiring land for the landless people. The white farmers peg the price of the farms at unaffordable market prices. Governments have finite finances to acquire land on behalf of the landless. Granted that not everyone wants to farm, but shelters have to be built on land.

Then there is the perennial problem of unfair land ownership patterns that are slanted on racial and ethnic lines. The white, Indian and Asian races came to Southern Africa much later than the San, Khoikoi and earlier Bantu groups. Hence, one has to convince persons whose land was seized from them, at one time in history, to buy the same piece of land back from the occupier.

For the World

Models of land reform programs can be gleaned from selected Asian and South American countries. The Japanese land reform program of 1954 imposed a ceiling on land holdings of one hectare. The land owners were compensated in cash and development bonds. In the course of the reform, the actual tillers were given full ownership rights for the land holdings they had previously cultivated and received subsidized mortgage. The key factors for the success of the reform were: a well developed extension service, good financial backing, sound land and production records, and an efficient bureaucracy.

In Taiwan, the 1953 land reform program placed a ceiling of one hectare to a farmer. The former land owners were compensated in industrial bonds which they invested in urban industrial and commercial zones. Productivity rose by 25% in four years. The country is self sufficient in food, and agricultural products.

In 1981 Vietnam enacted laws that broke up large collective farms into small family units. Incentives for individual farmers included recognized land use, and title to land. The reforms transformed Vietnam from a food deficit into a food surplus country. The small family units have increased the industrial and commercial crop out put such as rubber, coffee, tea, coconut, fruit and vegetables.

A crucial factor for the success of the land reform program in South Korea has been the thorough involvement and support of local people in land administration. In the course of the land reform 70% of the agricultural land was distributed to deserving farmers with a ceiling of three hectares per farmer. Former land holders were given an extra hectare. The former land owners were compensated with hard cash, bonds for urban areas and an extra hectare of land.

Moreover, the land issue continues to be a worldwide socio political issue. Countries like Bolivia in South America, have, as of June 2006, embarked on a, similar to Zimbabwean, controversial land redistribution exercise with obvious catastrophic fall outs as experienced in Zimbabwe. Lessons should be drawn from the Zimbabwean disastrous experience, and case study.

However, crucial good lessons can be learnt from the Asian experience and case studies. Land reform must be carefully planned, designed and implemented with small but viable family units at the core. Former land owners of large scale farms should be fully and adequately compensated for their land and developments. This should be done through a mixture of hard currency, bonds and part of the land itself. Owner operated family farms are generally more efficient in the use of land, inputs, skills development, and motivation. Secure property rights especially title to land promote long term investment, sustained interest in resources conservation, transfer of skills, and land use education. Another important lesson is that a well thought out land reform program leads to sustainable growth, development, productivity, poverty eradication and self sufficiency.

Beyond Land Acquisition

Land acquisition, tenure and poverty eradication should go beyond land itself. The effects of the problem manifest themselves on the economy, the environment, the geo politics, health and education. There is need for fundamental changes in the economy to correct the consequences of misguided macro economic and structural policies. There is need to go towards a different agro based paradigm. There is need to balance the principle of economies of scale and a land reform program which favours small scale holdings. Small scale holdings tend to employ more people, generate more income and increase productivity (IFAD, 2001).

The agrarian reform paradigm shift advocated above should include:

1.   Progress monitoring indicators based on agreed objectives and micro management strategies, access to farm capital, inputs and implements
2.   A comprehensive policy and regulatory framework , institutional development, and capacity building
3.   Land use planning, and extension services
4.   Civic, ethical and human rights education programs
5.   Civic participation and self development, especially for marginalized people
6.   Reliable, efficient water for supplementary irrigation
7.   Education systems that seriously encompass agriculture in the curricula. There is need to spread the network of young and adult education, awareness of land utilization, fair distribution of land resources, sustainable resource management and development.

Above all, it should be based on moral, ethical and international legal considerations.

Tasks for Discussion

Suggest and justify three strategies your country can implement in a land reform program for the landless. What would be the major problems related to the program?

Modernisation, Colonialism, and Under-development

Modernisation is a relative and contentious term. It depends on a number of factors such as time frames, point of view, socio-culture and economic inclination. In 2000 B.C. Egypt was more modern that Europe. What Egypt boasted of, Europe had nothing to show for it. Scientific developments like writing, alphabet, paper, mathematics, construction of pyramids, the wheel, mummification, moments in irrigation, were advances far superior to European ignorance, backwardness in food production, transport, illiteracy, and even lack of personal hygiene. Mutubuki (2003). But today, Europe would boast of space travel, writing technologies, communication networks, while Africa lags behind. The Japanese beat Europe in many of these inventions and technologies. On the other hand cynics would argue that there is nothing that is new under the sun. It is a matter of themes and variations of the same.

Modernisation theories link modernisation with change. Change is regarded as promoting greater productivity, creativity and work efficiency. People develop strategies to cope with problems and challenges of life. So, problems of life, and living, bring change and developments that influence norms, values, language, behaviour, attitudes and beliefs. McLelland (1983) says that for a society to become modern, it must be composed of an enlightened population, aware of contemporary issues, values and behaviours. This is why certain societies have attained higher levels of social and technological organisation than others. Hence, schooling plays a pivotal role for transforming a traditional society into a modern one.

When colonialist powers came to Africa, in the 17th century, they found Africans having lost their previous splendour, the Great Zimbabwe civilisation, for example, having crumbled. There were internecine wars, raids and looting. The colonialists added misery to this state of affairs, exploited it, and benefited materially, socially, politically and religiously. Colonialism affected the lives of the colonised immensely in many ways: materially, socio economically, socio culturally and politically.

They went on further to carve up Africa into small controllable states among the European powers. The Berlin Conference, of occupying European countries held in 1884, partitioned Africa into nation states. The motives were that European industrialisation needed raw materials and resources. For details on the partition of Africa see figure 1 below.

A number of strategies were used to occupy the African peoples. Social tools were used such as explorers who used the compass and map, the missionaries who used religion and the Christian Bible, the hunter/prospector who used prospecting equipment and the gun. Occupation saw economic, military and political tools being used, such as treaties and concessions, wars and eventual domination.

These states were made dependent on the colonial power for governance, economic activity and communication. The states were fragmented in such a way that they could not be viable economically. Most of the states were land locked with no direct access to the sea. These colonial boundaries have remained despite their artificiality and absurdity. The South African Apartheid regimes perfected it in the form of Bantustan states. This process and practice is called balkanisation. The states in the Balkan peninsular of north-eastern Europe were artificially carved up, by the then European powers, to stop them from becoming strong military states. Up to now the Balkan states are finding it difficult to un-bundle, and become socio economically independent.

This state of affairs has continued even long after the colonialists have left, in the form of neo-colonialism. When things get to a crunch in developing countries, the former colonial nations come in directly through a number of ruses. As recent as 2011 regional grouping such as ECOWAS in West Africa appealed to the United Nations Security Council to intervene in the Ivory Coast civil war. Before the ink was dry on the Security Council resolution, France, the former coloniser, was in Ivory Coast ousting Laurent Ggabo, and sent him to the International Crime Court at the Hague. Not long ago the Arab League appealed to the UN Security Council to intervene in Libya's civil war. Again France, the former colonial master, spearheaded an attack by NATO forces on Libya, ending in the ouster, and death of Muamar Gaddafi. In 2013 France yet again sent in crack units to deal with insurrections by Islamic professed fighters bent on taking over government in Mali. Former colonisers have the advantage of having linguistic, socio cultural, economic, political, military, and intelligence links with the former colonies.

In a more subtle form, African socio culture has been under relentless attack. Culture, language, religion, dress, values and norms remain those of the colonialists. After generations of European exposure African socio culture continues to be controlled by remote control by European norms and values.

All this can lead to problems of development. Resources such as raw materials, minerals, humans, industrial and commercial enterprises would continue to flow out of developing countries to developed nations. This undermines the quality and quantity of life for the former colonised people. This continued exploitation of developing countries' resources leads to under-development.

Institutions in developed countries further sharpen and deepen the exploitation of developing countries' resources. We are going to look at Trans National Corporations, the International Monetary Fund, the World Bank, Aid agencies, and debt, as they affect developing countries.

Trans National Corporations

Trans National Corporations are mega businesses operating in and across nations. They grew from multi national companies to larger mergers covering energy, technology, mining, food production and processing, manufacturing and commerce. They are huge capitalist organisations operating trans-nationally. They have access to, and control, the world's vital resources. Hence, they wield a lot of social, economic and geo political influence and power. They are viewed as the invisible hand of capitalism. They are reputed to make or break presidents, the world over. They see the world as without borders. Examples of TNCs are Anglo American Corporation, UniLever, DeBeers, Rio Tinto, Coca Cola, Shell/British Petroleum, British American Tobacco, Glencore International, Cable News Network.

There are a number of positive contributions made by Trans National Corporations. They provide foreign direct investment which is necessary for socio economic growth. They initiate and develop capital investment, capital projects, infrastructure like rail, road, ports, hospitals, schools, energy and water reticulation. In the process they create a lot of employment. All this initiates a multiplier process generating more income resulting in the growth of ancillary enterprises such as banking and insurance. Because of their capital resources and social networks they can call upon tremendous investment opportunities. Their presence and economic activities contribute to the country's fiscal revenue through direct and indirect taxation. Management and entrepreneurial skills learned from TNCs, through education and training, are important in terms of human capital.

But the power to switch investments and production around the globe has weakened the power of host governments and labour movements. Barnard and Burgess (1996) complain that TNCs are responsible for the perpetuation of global inequality on a large scale for their advantage, increasing the gap between the poor and the rich. Their motivation for profit making, propel them to exploit natural resources with little regard to depletion and pollution of the environment. Furthermore, their resource extraction centres, like mining, manufacturing spawn social and health pathologies such as prostitution, drug taking, gambling, crime and violence. The TNCs' exploitation of natural resources through mining, agriculture and manufacturing has displaced, marginalised and alienated local people. Their control of world mass media and information technology makes them dominate the global flow and dissemination of knowledge, skills, ideas, attitudes, and culture of consumerism of their products. (Applerouth and Edles (2008).

TNCs have a tendency to engage expatriate staff in key areas ensuring that incomes generated are kept within a certain privileged group. On the other hand locals would provide a pool of cheap labour, usually semi skilled. Coupled with this practice is the use of intensive production methods utilising technology rendering manual labour irrelevant. All this would hinder transfer of knowledge and skills to the locals.

TNCs also have a tendency to transfer pricing, and market locations, where they shift resources and production between countries so as to benefit from lower wages, taxes and regulations. In the process they contribute to national and world poverty especially in developing countries. A typical case is Glencore International mining and commodity dealing trans-national company with headquarters in Switzerland. Through a series of subsidiary companies it trades commodities by selling its products to itself at rock bottom prices avoiding paying taxes, and banking its profits in tax havens such as Switzerland. A sorry example is Glencore's operations in Zambia. Glencore owns and operates Mopani Copper Mines on the Copper Belt. In 2012 it contributed 7% to Zambia's GDP in taxes and wages but made US$7 billion through inside trading through its subsidiary companies. Through its operations in Zambia, MCM contributed to pollution and environmental degradation, leaving locals with lung and body illnesses, in spite of the fact that there is the Zambian environmental protection agency. Besides, MCM is alleged to have contributed to Zambia's social problems through corrupt practices that swallowed in Zambia's former presidents Frederick Chiluba and Rupiya Banda.

The above illustrates the tip of the ice berg, or to use an African expression, the ears of a hippo in water, of TNC's continuation with neo colonial plunder of developing countries' resources, leaving the poor nations poorer.

Though TNC's are known to create investment opportunities, employment and social amenities, these are at huge costs to the developing countries. Critics argue that developing countries are better off without the socio economic mega ticks in the form of TNC's.

TNCs are also known to abandon obsolete, or unprofitable, locations and enterprises leaving behind empty shells and gaping holes in the ground, as they leave for better pastures.

The World Bank

The World Bank was set up in 1944 in Bretton Woods, New Hampshire in the USA in 1944. It was intended to rebuild capital markets following the destruction of the 2nd World War. So the World Bank's role was concerned with financing reconstruction and development through the construction of national infrastructure such as rail, road, port, dams and power grids. By supporting such national projects, through funding and technical support, the World Bank believed that it would bring about increases in productivity, out put, incomes and self sustaining economic growth and development.

The World Bank consists of two organisations both concerned with lending finance for development projects. The two organisations are

The International Bank for Reconstruction and Development (IBRD) which lends money, at commercial interest rates, to governments, or private firms guaranteed by their governments

And the International Development Association (IDA) which lends money called credits to the poor countries on concessionary terms. The repayments periods are longer that the IBRD loans and are almost interest free.

Portfolio Facilities for Disbursement of Loans

Loans are often made in the form of Special Drawing Rights (SDRs). These are artificial world liquid assets that are accepted in payment of debts. About 2% of the world reserves are made up from SRDs. There are four portfolio facilities for disbursement of loans. First, there is the Stand-by Arrangements (SBA). These are loans to countries experiencing short term balance of payment problems. The loan is at the market, commercial rate of interest. The repayment period is from 3 to 5 years. Surcharges apply to high access levels. The second portfolio is called the Compensatory Financing Facility (CFF). The financial terms are the same as those applying to the SBA but with no surcharge. The CFF is intended to assist countries with fluctuating commodity prices. The third facility is the Extended Fund Facility (EFF). This provides balance of payments support to countries experiencing balance of payments problems. The EFF involves large amounts of finance and is payable from 4 to 10 years. The fourth is called the Supplemental Reserve Facility (SRF). It is a large scale, short term loan to emerging market economies experiencing massive outflows of capital due to sudden loss of market confidence. The loan attracts 3 to 5% surcharge and is payable over 2 years.

Up until the 1970s World Bank lending was concentrated on building energy and transportation infrastructure like the construction of the Kariba Dam on the Zambezi river. However, the poor economic performance of many developing countries led to change of approach by the World Bank. The different approach involved identifying specific needs of regions within less developed countries. The Bank targeted small scale projects of a diversified nature such as food production, private health care, education, safe water and sanitation. Global corporations took advantage of the loans to work on water and sanitation reticulation.

Because of problems of corruption and misplaced investment the Bank loans have been tied to stringent conditions covering tender procedures, identifying and planning the projects, monitoring the progress of the financed project, and checking on quality imperatives. Other conditions linked to the loans included structural adjustment programmes such as full cost recovery of services such as health, education; privatisation of commerce, mines, and industry; cuts in civil service employment; streamlining education levels to concentrate on basic education. These became unpopular with developing countries which thrived on populist voter policies.

The International Monetary Fund

The International Monetary Fund is a sister organisation of the World Bank. It is situated on the town of Bretton Woods in New Hampshire in the United State of America. It was initiated in 1947 in response to the socio economic circumstances that had developed because of the 2nd World War. What worsened the problems was that countries were engaged in damaging trade fights using competitive devaluation and protectionism.

The IMF performs management functions for the World Bank. The World Bank performs the functions of a bank, and the IMF that of a manager. Originally the IMF was set up to perform three basic functions. The first function was to oversee a system of fixed and adjustable exchange rates. The second function was to promote currency convertibility to facilitate world trade. The third function was to facilitate the World Bank as the lender of the last resort to countries experiencing short term balance of payment problems. In 1971 the first function lapsed after the collapse of the fixed exchange rate system. In its place came the supervision of member countries' economic policies and problems. This last but important function has become the major business of the IMF.

The Workings of the IMF

Some of its work has been covered above. A country has to apply for membership of the IMF. Each member pays a subscription or quota to the Fund in gold reserves, or internationally accepted currency. The more a country contributes the more it can borrow in time of need. In addition, the amount a country contributes determines the number of votes it has. In other words this determines the amount of control a country has over IMF policy, election of officials, especially its chief executive. The USA has 70 votes, Britain 55, France 60, Japan 56 and Germany 45, whilst South Africa has 7 and Zambia has 1. Members can borrow from the Fund on a wide range of terms. Members can borrow back their quota on a no strings attached basis. But a country cannot borrow more that three times its quota. If a country borrows above its quota it has to agree to certain stringent conditions. The more it borrows the tougher the conditions. The Fund's total quota is US$3 trillion.

It should be noted that no major industrialised economy has borrowed from the Fund since 1972. The Fund's major clients are less developed countries and transition economies.

The IMF has a lot of repayment problems with borrowers from less developed countries. Misplaced funds, corruption, mismanagement and governance issues make it very difficult for borrowing countries to pay back the loans. Failure to adhere to the loan conditions affects the sources of future funds from organisations such as the World Bank, donor countries and other multilateral donor communities. Furthermore, the burden of debt repayments and the tough conditions required take a heavy toll on defaulting countries' development and reduction of poverty.

In mitigation, the IMF and the World Bank launched the Highly Indebted Poor Countries Initiative (HIPCI) in 1996. It was meant to create a framework for all creditors to provide debt relief to the world's poorer, and most indebted nations. This would reduce the inhibitors on socio economic growth and poverty reduction. The initiative was revised in 1999 to provide three key enhancements. More countries became eligible for deeper and greater debt relief. This also permitted the affected countries to receive faster interim debt relief. The freed resources, in form of debt relief, were to be used to support poverty reduction strategies in the countries concerned.

To be considered for HIPC Initiative assistance a country should face an unsustainable debt burden beyond available debt relief mechanisms. The debtor country should establish atrack record of reform and sound policies through IMF and World Bank supported programmes. The country should have developed a poverty reduction strategy paper (PRSP) through a broad based participatory process. This process consists of two stages. Stage one is the decision point. The first step here is to carry out a debt sustainability analysis to determine the debt relief needs of the country and a poverty reduction strategy paper (PRSP). Once the IMF and World Bank formally decide a country has made sufficient progress in meeting the criteria for debt relief, the international community commits to reducing debt to the sustainability threshold. The second stage is the completion point. In order to receive the full reduction in debt available, the debtor country should establish a further track record of good performance under IMF and World Bank supported programmes. The length of this second period depends on three things: One, the satisfactory implementation of key policy reforms agreed to at the decision point; the maintenance of macro economic stability, and three the adoption and implementation for at least one year of the PRSP. Once a country has met these criteria, lenders are expected to provide the full relief committed at the decision point.

As a hedge against the effects of world recession, and socio economic emergencies, the IMF and World Bank have put in place a Firewall Fund. This is a rainy day fund to guard against the effects of a down turn in world economy. It is an economic fire fighting extinguisher.

Non Governmental Organisations (NGOs)

Non Governmental Organisations, sometimes referred to as multilateral institutions, are private organisations that provide development assistance to communities, groups and societies. The organisations are varied and diverse. They may be United Nations based, charities, religious groups, groups of health care workers, human rights activists, agricultural specialists or environmental conservationists. Examples of international NGOs are World Food

Programme, Care International, Action Aid, Plan International, Amnesty International, the Red Cross, Transparency International, Oxfam, Practical Action, Medicin San Frontiers (Doctors Without Borders). There has been a proliferation of national or local NGOs that provide development assistance from within the country concerned. These have tended to be of a dubious nature.

NGOs are often voluntary organisations that work at grassroots level within communities focusing on specific areas of assistance such as emergency famine relief, health or disease outbreaks, poverty relief, environmental protection, empowering marginalised groups, protection of human rights, providing micro financial credit. NGOs are not supposed to be politically or ideologically tied. So they are generally trusted by the public who appreciate their work with the poor and disadvantaged.

However, NGOs have been criticised for patronising recipients and choice of projects. NGO officials have been accused of using large chunks of aid resources to their own creature comfort such as luxurious accommodation, luxury vehicles, hefty salaries and benefits. Because of the attractive life style, the officials delay completion of projects to prolong their stay in the countries concerned. Hence, they have been accused of encouraging the dependency culture among the recipients. Governments and municipalities have been known to wait for NGOs to come in and provide services which they are supposed to provide themselves. In some instances governments have diverted budgeted funds to non essentials like luxury hotels, parliament buildings, arms of war and suppression.

Nevertheless, NGOs do tremendous work in alleviating poverty, disease, human suffering, refugee problems, environmental damage, and human rights violations. They play a vital humanitarian, philanthropic and developmental role in developing countries in particular, and the world in general.

Aid, Debt and Under-development

The term aid is a broad one. Aid refers to cash or in kind that are given to a recipient by a giver expecting repayment in one form or another. It can be in loan or grant form. Aid usually meets two criteria. It should be non commercial from the giver's point of view. It should be concessionary in terms of interest and repayment. Aid can be divided into public or official development assistance, and private development assistance. Public or official development assistance can be multilateral or bilateral aid. Private development assistance can be given by wealthy individuals, groups or Non Governmental organisations.

Aid is usually tied to certain conditions, written or unwritten. Tied aid by source means that the recipient must spend the aid resources on goods and services from the giver's place. Tied aid by project means that the giver requires the recipient to spend the aid on a specific project. Often it is to the giver's commercial or economic benefit.

Reasons for Giving Aid

Aid is given for a variety of motives ranging from humanitarian, ideological, political, strategic, and moral to economic interests. Self interest tends to run through most aid programmes. Aid, debt, bail outs, loans are linked to donor or giver's hidden agendas. The basic drive is the profit and benefit motive. It is what is called in the trade, the unfair cost of a hair cut. The donor, or giver, feels the receiver needs a hair cut which the recipient cannot afford. Say the cost of the hair cut is put at $3. The donor or giver spends $2 on administration costs, and own hair cut, leaving the recipient with $1. . At the end of the day the poor recipient carries the burden of repayment conditions plus interest and other charges on the total sum owing.

Economic reasons also dictate the purposes and functions of aid. The international product life cycle theory suggests that as industrially developed countries progress they have to off load excess, low quality and obsolete goods and services on less industrialised countries. Political and ideological reasons are also behind aid assistance. Aid is often designed to achieve political, strategic, ideological and religious motives. Aid is usually given to 'progressive and democratic' societies. Aid is also given to promote language, socio culture, education and technology. National security concerns often determine decisions on who receives aid.

The Benefits of Receiving Aid

As indicated above aid giving and receiving serve many purposes and motives. These range from economic, political to moral reasons. Countries seek and receive aid for socio economic reasons. The motive could be to improve the investment climate, develop human and resource capital, and to foster trade. Aid supplements lack of local resources such as foreign currency. It enables vital infrastructure development such as roads, ports, power generation and transmission grids. Less popular regimes in less developed countries view aid in terms of power and control of the restless populace. Often aid in form of military hardware provides the power base for suppressing opposition so as to maintain existing government in power.

Many people in less developed countries see the rich nations as having moral responsibility to provide aid to poor nations. They feel rich nations were once colonisers who became rich by exploiting resources from colonies. So it is incumbent upon the rich nations to redistribute the resources.

The Debt Boomerang

Aid has been part donation and part debt. Many developing countries accrued huge debts through unfavourable world economic conditions, misplaced investments, short sighted policies, corruption and a raft of governance problems. So the burden of debt has caused suffering and poverty. The debt burden also affects the rich nations as we shall see later in this chapter. Hence, it is in the interests of poor and rich nations to address the debt problem.

George, S. (2001) warned that there is going to be a debt boomerang effect for the rich and poor nations. Most of the arguments for debt relief, rescheduling and cancellation are based on the view that debt exacerbates poverty, human suffering, growth and development. The structural adjustment and macro economic stabilisation programmes, as conditions for multilateral and bilateral lending, often worsen the plight of debtor countries. When this happens both the rich world and the poor world reap a harvest of problems.

Debt and poverty cause unemployment and socio economic migration. Socio economic migration moves from poor to richer nations causing legal, social, refugee and humanitarian problems. The immigrants would be looking for a better life. Debt can lead to social instability, riots and violent demonstrations. Social and political instability can lead to civil war. If the conflict develops into civil war, the rest of the world may be dragged into the dispute for economic, political, ideological and strategic reasons. Some less developed countries may degenerate into failing states with war lords on land, sea and air, making life unsafe in the world.

There is also the drugs argument. Debt and poverty can make some individuals and groups to look for income from illegal production and sale of drugs like cocaine, opium and heroin. Some farmers would go into the lucrative production of drugs like the opium poppy. Drug lords can appear and cause social, legal and criminal havoc. The drug market is usually the rich nations. The consumption of drugs creates serious social and economic costs to the rich consuming nations.

There is also the environmental argument to the debt and poverty burden. Debt induced poverty causes people in less developing countries to recklessly exploit natural resources, fauna and flora in an unsustainable way. This leads to serious reduction in the biodiversity of the planet earth.

Debt Relief, Rescheduling and cancellation

Increased global awareness of the effects of debt on socio economic development and poverty reduction in poor countries, and the realisation of the detrimental effects on creditor countries as well, have led to pressure to review the debt crisis. This pressure has led to a number of measures, some less palatable than others.

Debt restructuring involves restructuring the debt so that it becomes bearable, with concessionary terms. The 2003 Toronto terms of the Paris Club (a grouping of bilateral donors) gave the creditor countries the option of partial cancellation of official debt by reducing terms of interest rates and rescheduling the debt by prolonging the pay back period. This offered some but not all the relief.

Debt forgiveness and rescheduling was proposed by the Brady Plan. The plan proposed that debtor countries be partially forgiven their commercial debts if they borrowed more from the IMF and World Bank to repay the remaining commercial debt. The IMF stringent conditions imposed on the debtor countries made the plan unattractive to the debtor countries. They felt it was an invidious choice of moving from the frying pan into the roaring fire.

Debt for equity, or nature swaps were also offered by creditor countries to debtor nations. Debt for equity swaps meant the commercial debt of the debtor country could be bought by a private company in a market place and exchanged for shares in a local state owned asset such as railways, energy generating company, telecommunications. This was opposed by debtor nations who felt robbed of their national assets. It was a case of paying Peter to pay Paul. The proposed debt for nature swap involved the commercial being purchased by the World Wildlife Fund, or a group of wealthy individuals, or NGOs, restructured in such a way that discounts were made against the debt for environmental conservation projects. Debtor countries felt emasculated leading to loss of face and sovereignty.

The Jubilee 2000 campaign advocated that debts for developing countries be cancelled altogether given that they had repaid exorbitant sums of money to the lenders. The debts seemed to stubbornly remain unpaid. The Paris Club agreed to write off 67% of the poor countries' debt and reschedule the remaining 33% on more concessionary terms. The group of eight world's richest nations (G8), at their 2005 meeting in Gleneagles, U.K, proposed that the 18 poorest countries should have debt relief. Debtor countries which have reached completion point within the HIPC initiative would receive 100% debt cancellation. This would cover $40 billion of debts owed to the World Bank via IMF, and the African Development Bank. The funds so owed would be provided by the G8 and the IMF. On paper this looked like a lot of money. But in real terms it would cost the G8 less than 1% of their Gross National Income. It would be equivalent to 40.10 cents per person per week in the G8 nations. It is akin to the poor Lazarus receiving crumbs from the rich nations' dining table.

The Development of Under-development

There are so many factors that cause under-development especially in less developed countries. As we have seen in the previous chapters there are a plethora of causes of under development. Manifestations of under-development include debt, poverty, dependency, unemployment, hunger, malnutrition, disease, illiteracy, school drop outs, socio-political instability, migration and crime. Under-development refers to the unpalatable conditions of people and country lacking basic needs and facilities. It is a state of having very low levels of socio economic productivity, technological sophistication, political prudence and well being. Under-development can occur where resources are not used to their socio economic potential. Education can be instrumental in the alleviation of poverty, hunger, unemployment, socio political repression, ignorance, illiteracy and obscurantism. Curricula, pedagogies, didactics, theory and praxis should empower learners for the real world of life.

For discussion

Discuss the claim that the world would be a better place without the World Bank, IMF and NGOs. Discuss the relationship between poverty and dependence syndrome.

Social, Cultural and Political Conflict in Africa and Under development

Almost all African states came out of colonialism with promises and hopes of eradicating differences among their people such as inequality, ethnicity, race, gender, political affiliation, religion and ideology. Independence, in every case, was greeted with euphoria, great expectations of freedom, peace, tranquillity, equality, socio economic growth and development. This was not to be, due to a number of factors ranging from social, cultural, religious to political dissolution.

The world is drenched in human blood, and so is Africa. The story of Africa is one of strife, wars, the slave trade, genocide, coups and counter coups. Africa seems to be angry with itself. Africa leads the world in internecine wars spewing refugees into, and around, itself. The colonial and neo colonial legacies have led to petty jealousies, mistrust and artificial barriers and boundaries. African nations profess to protect sovereignty, power and space while foreign interest individuals and groups loot Africa's resources overseas.

Analysis of African social life shows that most Africans have a propensity to spend time, effort, funds and resources on social activities and events. Socio cultural activities and events tend to take centre stage at family, group and national levels at the expense of development. A lot of time, energy, money and resources are put into social events such as funerals, weddings, birthdays, church services, rain making ceremonies and other cultural festivities, despite their unproductive nature. At national level socio cultural priorities gobble funds, time, effort and resources on state funerals, festivals, galas, conferences and workshops. Funds and resources are diverted from socio economic development projects to grandiose buildings such as hero's acres, conference centres, state houses, hotels, stadiums and prestigious mansions. These establishments show how inclined Africans are towards social investment, which brings very little economic returns.

This socio cultural investment runs counter to socio economic investment. Though socio cultural investment seems to pay dividends in times of hardship and crises it does not guarantee socio economic security. If there is no economic productivity people cannot share poverty.

The traditional African social structure, norms and values have played their part in the dissolution process. Family, group and totemic dynamics played into the new Eurocentric fabric distorting loyalties, alliances and social formations. Most African families then were largely extended to include related groups by blood and marriage. These merged into ethnic linkages that cut across geographical areas fomenting discriminating, segregating and separating functions and processes. Cultural, religious and economic differences wove dangerous strands into the fabric of society. Fertile grounds for division, differences and clashes then came into play. Past, and historical, events and episodes took a new and frightening dimension leading to ethnic and religious intolerance. Fears, real or imagined, led to ethnic clashes that eventually led to civil wars. In worse scenarios civil wars led to war lords and ethnic cleansing crusades such as Sudan's Darfur, Rwanda's Hutu/Tutsi genocide and the Congo internecine wars.

Political conflict in Africa stems from a number of factors such as socio culture, ethnicity, obscurantismo and governance. The first post colonial regimes were led and run by African nationalists who had been schooled in European institutions, curricula, and world view. In short they had imbibed neo colonialism. They had surreptitiously emulated and envied the colonial system and its trappings. They had developed a sneaking admiration of the white man's ways of life. They wore the colonialist shoes, on the wrong feet, in the wrong way. They, in the main, inherited the colonial socio economic, political and legal systems. Any changes made were cosmetic. The leadership went to live in former colonial accommodation, rode their vehicles, kept their prisons and legal frameworks. Meanwhile the ordinary people continued to live in squalid conditions, eking out a living of bare necessities. Those who dared protest were thrown into prisons with little legal considerations. The same prisons were now infested with vermin and over crowded than before.

African nationalist parties and their leadership have not been able to accommodate views different from their own. Ethnic differences have been exploited to advance political ends. Socio cultural practices such as roles of chiefs have been used to control the restless population. Opposition parties and their leaders have been intimidated, harassed and banned. The ruling nationalist leaders have stubbornly refused to relinquish power, and instead use nationalist slogans to indoctrinate people in order to dominate them. Fanon in Chung and Ngara (1985) observed that nationalist parties mobilise people with slogans of independence. But when they are questioned on socio economic programmes of the state that they are clamouring for, they are incapable of explaining. The reason is that they are precisely ignorant of the economy of their own country. This means that African nationalist leaders have been obsessed with maintaining themselves in power rather than planning for future development. The major part of the reason is that they fear exposure of their corruption, looting of resources and crime that had become endemic during their rule. This lack of commitment to socio economic development has made under-development a permanent feature in most of Africa.

Another socio cultural factor that contributes to Africa's under-development is the condescending behaviour and deference to wrong, illegal acts by political leaders. Political leaders and their parties get away with murder, crime, corruption and immoral behaviour because good people keep quiet. In the process political cabals and desperadoes run and ruin the economy and country's resources. Their interests dictate the nature, pace and direction of the state and economy, and not the needs of the people. Dininio (1999) observes that public officials, and office of president, wield wide authority in government, defence, state security and education with very little accountability. This leaves a lot of room for abuse of power, corruption and ineptitude. It can be concluded that African leaders and their parties have not been concerned about national socio economic development; rather they are obsessed with personal enrichment, power, dignity and prestige.

Yet another problem lies with what socio psychologists call the normalcy bias. In times of crises people tend to go into serious denial. The normalcy bias refers to people's natural reactions when facing a crisis; it could be personal, political, financial or social. In other words, people believe that since something has never happened before, as far as they know, it never will happen. Almost all people believe so. It seems to be just human nature. The tragedy is that it makes people unable to deal with a disaster, once it has occurred. Even before the disaster happens, it is difficult for people to prepare for, and deal with something they have never experienced before. Events move much faster than people can imagine. But people can simply refuse to see the evidence that is right in front of their faces, because it is unlike anything they have experienced before. Perceptive people warn others of impending danger, but in vain, until it is too late. A tragic example is the Jewish holocaust under Hitler's Nazi Germany.

There were thousands of wealthy, brilliant, cultured and cosmopolitan Jews in Germany who watched and ignored Hitler's rise to power, without using their tremendous influence to stop him. Even as late as the Nazis started to arrest, beat, tax, rob, jail and kill Jews for no reason other than that they were socio culturally different, many Jews remained complacent. They stayed in Nazi Germany believing that things would get better, until it was too late. (Biggs, 1975). There are so many tragic examples of normalcy bias in the world, where, and when, good people do nothing for wrong things to happen. They seem to say as long as it is not happening to them directly, they must be safe… until the perpetrators of injustice come for them as the next victims. A lot of wrong, evil things are happening in the world, with good people watching. Genocides, crimes against humanity are attended to, albeit too late.

Under performance by the political institutions in most of Africa leads to socio economic melt down which cripples education, health and social services. This can lead to failing economies, instability and failed states. It is evident that under-development in Africa is, in the main, caused by factors emanating from the African states themselves. Conflict in many African countries, leads to socio economic stagnation, stunted growth and ultimately under-development. Wrong policies and investment decisions taken by governments scare away investors leading to unemployment and poverty.

Africa and world political and social turmoil continues

Africa, and the world, is so full of socio political turmoil that adversely affects people, fauna, flora and the environment. The world is full of conflict, wars, human rights violations, deaths, rape, refugees and violence. Everyone, and everything, has the right to life and peace, the United Nations' organs declare. But alas no one seems to notice or care. The theories and explanations offered in this book try to explain the reasons and causes. According to the historian, Richard Hofstadter (2010), the main cause of socio political turmoil in the world is ideological and political extremism. This is a strong force he calls the paranoid style. He describes the paranoid style as evoking heated exaggeration, suspicion and conspiratorial fantasy. It is the use of paranoid modes of expressions by more or less normal people that make the phenomenon significant. These include the identification of an enemy, the exaggeration of that enemy in the popular consciousness, accusations of conspiracy, and unwillingness to compromise, fear mongering and manipulation. The paranoid style sees only good and evil, nothing in between: a black and white world with no room for grey. People get attacked, shot, hatred for certain individuals, or this or that group.

Political rhetoric becomes the order of the day. Rhetoric involves strategies used to construct persuasive arguments in socio political debate. These are words of expected action that get people moving in a political direction. The words are used to incite people, to hate, blame, label and factionalize. The press and cyber media are used to convey socio political paranoia and opportunism.

Africa, Asia, America and Europe are full of paranoid style in form of politics, religion, race, colour, gender, ethnicity and tribe. Sadly, there seems to be little regard for human dignity, the achievement of equality, non racialism, non sexism, and everyone's right to life.

The Way Forward

People driven programmes should be carried out to rid society of corruption, intolerance, crime and unethical practices. Ordinary people should liberate themselves from the culture of condescension and deference to dictatorial and autocratic leadership. The normalcy bias syndrome should be replaced by collective social action. Leaders must be made to account for their behaviour, decisions and direction of the whole nation state. People driven constitutions, legal systems, socio economic programmes and development projects must be put in place. Governance and democratic structures should ensure that the needs and interests of the majority, and minority, are catered for. Voting behaviour, which is characterised by voter apathy, intimidation, and fear, should be addressed through voter education. The role of education in the above mentioned processes and practices is vital.

Questions for Review

Examine African aspects of culture relating them to problems in development and education. Discuss Africa's governance weaknesses as they affect socio economic development. Analyse the assertion that Africa's source of under development is drought and bankruptcy of leadership. Illustrate instances of paranoid style experienced in your country. Indicate how they lead to social, economic and political turmoil.

Sub Saharan Africa is experiencing two forms of liberation: the first from colonial and racist regimes, and the second from the autocrats who followed the colonial regimes. In addressing the colonial legacy African governments had to manage two transitions. The first one was the tendency to regard the messianic psyche of the so called liberators themselves who tainted every criticism, no matter how constructive, as a threat to their power base. The second transition was the need to make and manage socio economic policies, and failure to recognise the place and role of international macro influences on economic growth and development. This led to individual and group denied freedom of expression and association. Because of lack of productive and manufacturing activities the country degenerate into under development.

Herbst and Mills (2012) say that African countries now have the potential to undertake a third liberation from political economies characterised by graft, crony capitalism, rent-seeking, predatory behaviour, state capture, corruption, elitism and social inequality. This third liberation will open up the socio economic space in which business can compete and develop the countries. There is the pressing need for Africa's leaders and interest groups to promote socio economic growth in their countries. There is need to create enabling environments for business and economic growth through good governance, provision of infrastructure for manufacturing and production, coupled with relevant education. A development roadmap should be put in place to chart strategies for economic take off. With the implementation and application of more responsive policies, and wisdom, the 21st century, beckons as the African century.

The Three Pillars of Development

For African countries to attain development status, they have to effectively meet the basics required by the people such as access to clean water, food, sanitation, health, education, shelter and other basic utilities. Following up on this is the need to work on the three pillars of an inclusive, peaceful and cohesive society. These are one: Peace and security. Two, there should be genuine development involving the vibrant youth, women and the marginalised. The emphasis here should be harnessing Africa's vast resources, adding value to them through manufacturing and production. Three, active application of the rule of law and human rights should be prioritised. These would translate into processes and procedures for democratic elections, governance, transparency and social justice. Africa, and the world, belong to their citizenry, especially the youth. The youth, who constitute half of Africa's population, should take the leadership mantle from social, economic and political dinosaurs, who unfortunately are obsessed with personal power, wealth, and fear of retribution from international justice. Needless to say, the International Court of Justice is not meant for Africa. It is meant for perpetrators of murder, rape, violence and injustice on ordinary and helpless citizenry. The Rome statute of the International Crime Court is a noble cause for justice, rule of law, equality and fairness. If there are any people involved in deviant behaviour, they should be made to account for their actions of commission and omission.

Above all, Africa should move away from the social and political practice of winner takes it all, relegating opposing views to the periphery of society. This practice inevitably leads to animosity, violence, social turmoil and civil strife. All this is catastrophic for socio economic growth and development.

The Fallacy of some of Africa's Socio- economic Boom

Africa consists of 55 countries with different economies, most of them woefully undeveloped. The GDP of all these 55 countries combined is barely higher than the USA' state of California. Because Africa's economies are so immature, the current boom is unbalanced and unsustainable. The boom can come to bust sooner than later. Some regions seem to be prospering, others are not. Some sectors are booming, while others are languishing. Some of Africa's energy, infrastructure, resource exploitation and consumer goods sectors are growing rapidly.

There are underlying drivers of this boom. Most of the investment in resources and infrastructure is being debt financed by foreigners. Essentially Africa is being vendor financed by China and India, which two countries have an insatiable appetite for primary resources. The other driver of the boom is easy money coming from the global money market seeking higher interest earnings on African project capital investment. The East African logistics projects on power generation, energy exploitation, ports, communication, railway lines and road networks have attracted lenders like Kuwait, Qatar and Saudi Arabia. The other driver is linked to absence of local investment capacity in these projects. Governments in Africa do not incentivise private savings and investment in their countries. Hence, financing remains with foreigners. . As a matter of fact the authorities put in place restrictions on economic freedom. Worse, government and securocrat leaders want to get on the economic act alone minus the average person. Hence, the boom benefits a few giving the false impression that it reaches the majority of the population. The most significant driver is the retail and wholesale boom in consumables such as cheap electronic goods, clothes, food and furniture. Again foreign based businesses make brisk business in cahoots with local powerful groups and individuals. Above all, investment in ports, power, energy rail and road ultimately end up lowering the cost of doing business for the mineral and resources sectors that need reliable power and efficient transport to ship output abroad.

The socio-economic boom will be short lived because Africa's primary resources will run out leaving Africa with gaping holes, poor, with gleaming infrastructure and half built projects. Projects that looked profitable will be revealed as poor investments. Because the wealth of the boom would have gone to foreigners and a few powerful locals, poverty levels would rise as social indices like unemployment, hunger, disease and destitution ravage the general population.

Africa's logistics boom is reminiscent of the colonial scramble for resources, in particular its raw materials. Africa's lack of socio-economic leadership, just as in the colonial era, aids the exploitation. Colonialists led by the likes of Cecil John Rhodes and De Beers sought to develop ports, roads and railway systems from Cape to Cairo to facilitate the movement of goods, raw materials and workers. Today, the same historical events are repeating themselves, this time around with the Chinese, Indians and Arabs.

Diversity across Africa

Of the 55 African countries there are variations in socio economic growth and development. Some have done better than others. Countries that are doing better than others are Angola, Botswana, Mauritius, Namibia, South Africa, and Uganda. Those not doing so well are Algeria, Liberia, Morocco, Malawi, Nigeria, and Zimbabwe. Countries like DRC, Sudan, Burundi, Libya suffer from wars and insurrections that destabilise their socio economic growth and development. Cote d'Ivoire and Zimbabwe have poor economies and social chaos. Both countries have been destroyed, Cote d'Ivoire by a civil war and Zimbabwe by its own government. Zimbabwe's socio economy is worse than that of a country at war. Poor domestic policies, incoherent policies demonstrate the vulnerability of African countries to the disastrous decisions of their own governments. A number of these countries do not mark workers' day on May 1, but vendors' days as their form of socio economic activity.

Suggested Sustainable Solutions to Africa's Development Prospects

The critical question to answer is infrastructure investment in Africa helping the development of manufacturing and productive industry; or is it merely cheapening the flow of mineral resources out of it? The boom should translate to the development of manufacturing and production industries. Africa's primary resources should be processed, value added and exported as final refined products. Invested capital should be converted into fixed productive capital that can continue to drive economic growth. Sustained economic growth and development should be based on diversification away from primary extractive industries, and move decisively towards manufacturing and productive industries. It is only through production that the African economic boom can be sustained for generations to come.

Overall, Africa has three enormous assets. One, a young population with exposure to high education, energy and motivation is a critical asset. If correctly brought into the system of governance, economy and development their involvement would be of tremendous benefit. Two, the abundant natural resources can be added value and lead to sustainable growth and development. Three, a potentially powerful budding private and public sector can catapult African economies to high levels of operations.

For Reflection

Do you think new players on the African economic field like the Chinese, Arabs and Indians have positive roles that benefit Africans? Suggest and justify three possible ways in which post-colonial Africa can shed off the burden of nationalist regimes.

Africa's Contribution to World Civilization, Development and Education

Abstract

Africa has seriously been marginalized in almost all spheres of life in the world. Great ideas, developments, technologies and civilizations have been presented as a preserve of the western world. Consequently, Africa has largely been ignored, and is widely viewed as a mere recipient and consumer of European education, thought, knowledge, religion and literature; in short civilization. So Africa should lament the few strands of history, , education and development that come packaged as African, when in fact they are Europe's conception and interpretations of what Africa should be. So, African scholars must endeavour to enter a serious paradigm shift in researching, projecting and publishing Africa's immense contribution to world civilization, education, thought, knowledge, and ultimately development.

This chapter attempts to show the world that Africa is, in fact, the cradle of world civilizations. Great civilizations and technologies that the world is enjoying are a product of Africa's great minds and hands. The historical design, documentary method and archival, archaeological cum anthropological evidences are used to trace and authenticate Africa's contribution. The immense contribution covers metaphysical culture, material socio culture, writing, scientific and technological discoveries and inventions, medicine, construction techniques and mathematics.

Introduction

It is the argument of this chapter that development cannot take root in a situation where education and development promote the fallacy of knowledge, technology and civilization emanating from the northern world. Yet Africa is the uterus and cradle of not only person-kind but of the knowledge cum technological base dating back to ancient Egypt, Nubia and Central Africa. The foundation knowledge and skills of writing, literacy, science, mathematics, technology, agriculture, medicine, philosophy and monotheism is rooted in Africa. (Mutubuki, 2003). All the while it should be borne in mind that the north has a lot to learn from Africa even today.

People from the north, especially the ancient Greeks and Romans came to Egypt to learn in the Grand Lodges of Heliopolis and Luxor. When they went back home they reproduced the knowledge they had gained in Africa, repackaged it as their own. (James, 1954). In other words, this was intellectual theft. For unequal acknowledgement, distribution and utilization of knowledge is a barrier to peaceful sustainable development. Only if there is equitable ownership of, and access to, knowledge will it be possible in the long term to balance the needs, interests and view points. For a map showing Egypt as the earliest and most enduring civilization, among others, see figure 2 on page 62. .

It is not said here that the ancient African scientists, mathematicians and technologists succeeded in unravelling the laws and principles of nature. Basically the knowledge base has not changed much, only the details have shifted. Duncan and Weston-Smith (1977), in The Encyclopaedia of Ignorance, tell us that compared to the pond of knowledge, our ignorance remains Atlantic. Indeed the horizon of the unknown recedes as we approach it. So many thanks go to the ancient Africans who helped on matters which lie on the edge of knowledge. They charted the teleological explanations of phenomena and their potential application to daily activities.

Hence, we should reject the dependency paradigm that the social structures, content and form of society, reflect images of the northern world systems. The systems promote northern world perspectives ignoring the noble southern ones. Though Africa should scan globally, it should emphasize local and indigenous knowledge infrastructure and hardware. Africa has been widely seen as a recipient of European civilization, thought, knowledge and religion.

Ancient Africans contributed immensely to empirical, metaphysical, axiological and technological knowledge. It is pertinent to point out that the whole of North Africa, at the time of the Egyptian civilization, was populated by dark skinned Africans who had filtered through from Nubia, South east Africa and central Africa. Arabs are not the original inhabitants of Egypt and North Africa. They only moved in, from the Saudi Arabian peninsula, in the 5th century AD. (Duboi, 1965). So the present day Arab population of North Africa has no claim to the achievements of ancient Africa, or any other African civilization. Diop (1975) tells us that Egypt, Egypto means black, is the land of the black people whose ancestors came from Central and East Africa, Ethiopia and the heart of Africa. Herodotus, the Greek historian of the 5th Century B.C. described the Egyptians as Africans with woolly and kinky hair.

Material/Physical Socio culture

Historical, archival and archaeological evidence supports the views expressed in this chapter. Egyptians, Nubians and East Africans contributed immensely to material, physical socio culture. They used collective intelligence and pioneered scientific, mathematical and technological discoveries and inventions. Through these knowledge, skill bases they built the magnificent pyramids and other structures. They were responsible for the many scientific, technological discoveries briefly described below (Diop, 1974, Mutasa, 1994).

The calendar

The Egyptian calendar began in 4241 B.C. Childe (1957) pointed out that it was the first recorded achievement of the application of numbers to accurately record observations. The Egyptian year had 365 days made up of twelve months each with thirty days, and five feast days at the end to make the count right. The 24 hour day started at mid night, with measurement of small intervals using sun dials and water clocks. They had three seasons of the year, the Inundation, , Cultivation and Harvest, each four months long. This calendar, which is critical to planning of socio economic activities, of 365 days established 6000 years ago is still with us today.

Astronomy and astronomical observations

The need to predict events controlling agriculture led to the growth of astronomy. The early Africans had tables of star culminations and star risings. They were capable of determining the azimuth of a star using a plumb line and a forked rod. Exodas, a Greek, went to Egypt to study planetary motion. Pythagoras spent 22 years in Egypt studying astronomy, geometry and the mysteries (Pappademos, 1991). One of the oldest astronomical observations, Namoratunga II, was uncovered in north western Kenya. It was built, and used, in 300 B.C. The Dogon people of Mali have been able to project and plot the orbit of the star Sirius A, invisible since the middle ages. The Europeans only discovered this star this century, long after the Dogon had known it existed. (Sirtima, 1991).

The five basic machines

The five basic machines, now extensively used in industry, the lever, pulley, wheel and axle, wedge and inclined plane were widely used by the early Africans in the construction of pyramids. Indeed, the first efficient irrigation instrument, the shaduf operated on the principle of moments and lever (Ben-Jochannan, 1971).

Agriculture and Irrigation

Some 18000 years ago, specialised farming based on irrigation techniques, was first undertaken by Africans in Egypt's western desert and the banks of the Nile river. They raised wheat, barley, lentils, chick peas, capers and dates. So successful was the agriculture that Greece and Rome relied on this African food basket for their survival. (Davidson, 1975).

Writing

This is one of Africa's greatest invention and heritage to the world. Africans invented the first alphabet, hieroglyphics, paper (papyrus scroll), pen and ink. They wrote for business, commerce, education and pleasure. The learned writings are the Moscow, Kahun, Ebers, Smith papyrus scrolls contain invaluable knowledge, skills and vital data. Writing meant mathematical, astronomical, scientific, agricultural, medical and statistical knowledge could be codified, stored, recorded, communicated, retrieved and exchanged accurately. So writing, pen, ink and paper revolutionised, and transformed the world of learning, business, industry and entertainment.

Chemistry

The word chemistry comes from the African name, Kemet, the ancient name for Egypt. When Greek scholars had learnt science in Egypt and were practising at home, they called their practice alchemy, which meant of Kemet. So brilliant at chemistry were the Egyptians that their knowledge of mummification cannot be imitated to date. Ramases II, known as Tutenkhamen, a contemporary of Moses (Moshe), is still intact, with Moshe's remains having fossilised. Their belief in life after life made them mummify the sleeping dead, and buid pyramids and tombs of immortal grandeur.

Medicine

The knowledge of chemistry led to brilliance in medicine. The Egyptians produced the world's first doctors, surgeons, medical texts and hospitals. Details from the Ebers, Kahun and Smith papyri show clearly that there was already medical specialization by 2500 B.C. Moshe and his Egyptian wife Zipporah attended Heliopolis, and Luxor schools of medicine respectively. Medical experts like Imhotep, and Merit Ptah were deified because of their contribution to medicine and healing. (Koka, 1989). Sais was the academic and professional centre of earth sciences, agriculture, cosmology and architecture.

Mathematics

Africans developed arithmetic, algebra, geometry and trigonometry for use in agriculture, and the construction of pyramids and burial tombs. They applied mathematical calculations related to the flooding of the Nile river, and in the division of land along the Nile Valley, the most precious land that existed at that time. Euclid, the so called father of geometry, and Diophantis, the so called father of algebra, were Africans who lived in Egypt when it was under the Greeks. (Kondo and Kondo, 1987).

Universities

Africans built the first universities in the world. They called these centres of learning, Grand Lodges. The Grand Lodges of Heliopolis, Sais and Luxor prided themselves with higher learning studies in mysteries, earth sciences and medicine. Heliopolis specialised in leadership, mysteries, miracles and universal truths. Its famous students were Moses, and much later Jesus of Nazareth, who graduated with masters' degrees cum laude. Luxor specialised in medicine, music and sculpture. One of its prominent students was Zipporah, an African lady medical doctor who later on married Moses. Sais specialized in earth sciences, surveying, architecture, geology, engineering, advanced mathematics and agriculture. People from all over Europe, Asia and Africa came to the Grand Lodges to study different areas of specialization. Socrates, Aristophanes, Plato, Pythagoras and Hypocrates were some of the most prominent Greek scholars to go to Egypt to study complex philosophical systems called mysteries, mathematics and medicine. Today these complex philosophies are studied under the guise of Greek philosophical thought and praxis; mathematical formula and scientific theories. (Bernal, 1987, James, 1954).

Iron and steel

When the whole of Europe was enveloped in ignorance and superstition, prominent African thinkers were busy working on inventions and technologies. The Africans were smelting iron and steel to make ploughs, hoes, axes, hammers, trowels, shovels, wheels and axles, spears, arrows and various tools. The oldest known iron furnaces were uncovered in Tanzania. Sertima (1991) and Davidson (1975) tell us that these furnaces produced high quality carbon steel, with temperatures in them reaching 1800 degrees Celsius, a temperature not achieved in European cold blast bloomeries until late 19th century.

Metaphysical Socio culture

Africa' contribution to metaphysical socio culture permeates three of the world's religions, that is, Judaism, Islam and Christianity. These religions are monotheistic. The birth of monotheism is found in the thought of Egyptians, Ethiopians and Nubians who collaborated in many ways, stages and ages in philosophical and scientific thought. (Duboi, 1965; Davidson, 1974). Monotheism has its origins in the teachings of the Egyptian pharaoh Akhenaton born in 1345 B.C.

Akhenaton promulgated the worship of one supreme god. That was an invisible, all powerful and formless being. The one God created the universe physically and in his heart, the seat of his mind, and actualized it through his tongue, the act of speech. (Bernal, 1987; Mutasa, 1994). This was known as the Mephite Theology that was practised in Egypt, and taught at Heliopolis grand lodge. Akhenaton was also a brilliant scholar and teacher at Heliopolis. The most prominent disciple of Akhenaton, and Mephite theology, was Moshe (Moses). Moshe, born in 1316 B.C. in Egypt, spread the monotheistic gospel against polytheism among the Israelites. He became instrumental in shaping Judaism.

Jesus of Nazareth went to Heliopolis and like Moshe studied Mephite theology, mysteries composed of meditation, secret sciences, numerical and geometrical symbolism, magic, myth and parables. (Khun, 1974; Koka, 1994). Though Jesus, as a Jew, remained in Judaism, his followers became Christian, followers of Jesus Christ. That is how Christianity was born. The old testament of the bible forms part of Christian theology, showing the link between the two religions.

Islam's monotheism strongly came from Egyptian and Judaic influences mainly because of their physical and geographical closeness. There are so many similarities between Islam, a new religion compared to the older religions, Mephite theology and Judaism.

The first Bible

Bernal, 1987; Kondo and Kondo, 1987, say that the first bible was written by Africans of the Nile Valley, Great regions of central and east Africa. The book was called'The Book of the Coming Forth by Day and Night,' pays tribute tothe Creator of all person-kind. It was written around 4000 B.C. whereas Exodus was written by Moshe in 1200 B.C. Khun (1976) an expert on the origins of early Christianity say s that the Christian bible, creation legend, ark and flood allegory, gospel Epistles and Revelations; are all transmissions of ancient Egypt's papyri scrolls by people who did not bother to acknowledge their sources. The bulk of what makes the bible, in particular the old testament, has not been original. For instance, there is very close similarity between the teachings of Pharaoh Amenemope (1300 B.C.) and king Solomon's teachings in the book of Proverbs (970 B.C.) Mutasa and Mutubuki, 1995.

The Ten Commandments

The ten commandments were a part of the 147 laws known throughout the learned world in Egypt centuries before Moshe's birth. The 147 laws were known as tne 'Negative Confessions. Koka, 1990. Moshe, a scholar from Egypt, taught mysteries, and knew all about the Negative confessions prior to the Mount Sinai experience. All he had to do was to sum up the most significant into 10 commandments or laws.

December 25th Festive Holiday

December 25th festive holiday is the day the Egyptian Sun god Ra was born, that is, 25th December 3000 B.C.Koka, 1990. So 25th December, practised mainly by Christians, has nothing to do with the birth of Jesus of Nazareth. It has always been an important holiday for ancient Egyptians, and those who benefitted from their civilization such as Greeks, Romans and Europeans.

The Removed (Lost) Books of the Bible

Some of the 18 books removed from the Bible at the Nicene Bishops' conference in 325 AD, included the books written by Jesus' elder brother James. The Aquarius Gospel of Jesus Christ, and The Book of Mary gave details of Jesus' life in Egypt, especially from the age of 12 up to 30. Egypt (Africa) played a significant role in Jesus' academic, spiritual and professional life. Ben-Jochanan, 1973. Jesus attended Heliopolis Grand Lodge and studied mysteries, and in addition priests and initiates were taught cardinal virtues of justice, prudence, fortitude and temperance. So Jesus learnt knowledge, skills, wisdom and philosophical thought from Africa, that equipped him for his missionary role.

As indicated above, Africa contributed immensely to metaphysical thought and socio culture but European civilizations sought to conceal it. Indecd, what passes as Greek philosophy is African mysteries plagiarized on a phenomenal scale. Sertima, 1982; Mutasa, 1991.

African Literature and its Influence on Thought

Literature can be viewed as a social institution which uses language as its medium. It is a social creation that that serves a triad function: the cognitive, utility and pleasure functions. The novelist can teach us more about human nature than the psychologist. Utility is its function in terms of the cognitive, as well as the historical, delineating the socio cultural heritage for a society. That heritage involves thought processes, words of wisdom, wit, advice, humour, social and political satire. Literature can be oral,, written, prose, verse and song. Africans excelled in the field of literature long before Europe could read and write.

Ancient African literature spans generations before Europe knew what literature was all about. The early Africans, living in Egypt, Ethiopia and Nubia had invented writing, alphabet, papyrus scroll and ink. They used all these for various purposes. Around 3000 BC there were the teachings of Kagemi, of Pta-hotep, and Kaires. These writings were researches into moral and ethical perfection. They were also searches for refined language. Obenga, 1992. The birth of poetic art came with Ipuwer's prophesies called Admonitions of an Egyptian Sage. The stories reveal the sad effects of the political and social changes which occurred in Egypt. The Dialogue of a Desperate Person and his/her Soul is a beauty in terms political and social attire. This is a classic soliloquy of a desperate person discussing with his/her soul on the sad opportunity of staying in the world of the living, where are now banished the values that made it attractive. Songs of the Harpist (2100 BC) is a collection of poems sung at funeral scenes. Mutasa, 1994.

Tales of the Oasian, the loquacious peasant, is one of the longest text of ancient Egypt. In this story, a peasant complains to superior authorities after being ill treated by unscrupulous local officials. What comes out are classic themes of justice, wisdom, duties and rights of the poor, disadvantaged, rich, rulers and gods. In Tales of the Westcar Papyrus, king Cheops (his head forms part of the Sphinix at Giza) converses with Dijedi, the magician , on matters ranging from magical tricks, political treachery, economic prudence to good governance. Other classical Egyptian texts include oral didactics like The Dead are Happier than I am, Life's variety. On the Eve of Krina, is an inspiring, cheering, priming, teaching and historical rendition. Mutasa, 1994.

So Africa, through its literature gave birth to most ideas in classic literature like the Bible, Greek mythology, Roman literature, and in turn western literature. Those Africans who invented writing in the first place, through the arts and sciences, bequeathed to humanity the rich literature for learning, teaching, utility, pleasure, and ultimately civilized thought.

The above summation of Africa's immense contribution to world civilization, knowledge, skills, education and development should form the basis for Africa's education, socio economics, politics and thought. This rich foundation is at risk of being lost in the mist of time, space, intellectual piracy and neo colonialism. Policy makers, teachers and experts in different fields should put in place proactive programmes of rediscovering, teaching, patenting, codifying and exchanging the rich African heritage. None but ourselves shall liberate our immense contribution from obfuscation, obscurity and neo colonialism.

Recommendations

The main recommendations of the chapter centre on the need to change and maintain the African and indigenous knowledge base. Local and indigenous knowledge and skills should be at the centre of school curricula, faculty courses in colleges and universities. Ancient Egyptian, Ethiopian and Nubian studies in science, mathematics, medicine, agriculture, cosmology, thought and so on should be at the core of education, economic growth and development. In other words, African education systems and curricula should reorient learners on the elements of Africa's knowledge, skills and experiences as a base. Philosophy and sociology courses should emphasize and underline Africa's contribution to metaphysical and material socio culture. Western thought should be placed in the context of its roots in African thought. Religious studies should have the correct perspective in tune with their origins in Africa. Science and technical courses should start on the basis of Africa's scientific and technological discoveries and inventions. Agricultural studies have to take into account Africa's experiences in irrigation, fertigation, animal husbandry, crop science and seed preservation. Medical courses should have basic studies relating to Africa's achievements in the medical field such as mummification, herbal therapies, hydro water treatment, intravenous cures. History texts need to emphasize and highlight Africa's endeavours in human thought, socio economic growth and development. Literature courses should be based on African literary prowess, its influence on thought and human action.

Acknowledgement and exchange of the rich African heritage to the world should be actively worked on through research and publication. A Pan African university, with satellite centres similar to ancient Egypt's Grand Lodges, should be established. Funds for these centres can be garnered from the citizenry of Africa, those in the diaspora, as well as well-wishers from the world.

Questions for Discussion

Suggest ways in which Africa's past heritage can be incorporated in education, science, and technology. In what fora should Africa's contributions be promoted?

Development and the Role of Education

Education is regarded as one of the vital factors in socio economic development. At the individual level, development implies increased skills such as reading writing and arithmetic. It also brings in concepts of freedom, choice, and motivation to be creative, inventive and manipulate. At the group level the individual capacities outlined above remain relevant. But there is an extension that brings in the capacity to regulate internal and external forces and relationships. According to Rodney (1972) a society develops socio economically as its members increase jointly their capacity for dealing with the environment. This capacity is dependent on the extent to which they understand the laws and forces of nature.

Development, like life, is a ladder; some people ignore it, some just carry it, some utilise it rung by rung to reach great heights, others attempt to climb it from the top. Each action, or lack of it, produces different results. It is the task of education to help people utilise the ladder of development, of life, to achieve desired heights.

In the process and practice of development, education fulfils many social purposes suh as transmission of knowledge, skills, socio culture and philosophical thought. So education is seen as a continuous creative process whose main aim is to develop the latent and manifest capabilities in human nature, and coordinate their expression for the enrichment and progress of society. In the same vein, education should lead to the discovery and perfection of one's capability by instilling commitment to serve the needs of the community. Hence, education must act as a potent instrument for profound social, economic and political transformation in the individual, group and society at large.

It is pertinent to observe that development and the role of education are guided by theories such as human capital, conflict and modernisation. Human capital theory is based upon the works of Schultz (1961) and Denison (1962). The two economists propounded that formal education is highly necessary and instrumental in the production capacity of a population. To them an educated population is a productive population. So an investment in education is an investment in the productivity of the population. They concede though that other factors like food, health and accommodation are also essential.

The conflict theory criticises the human capital theory. Bowles and Gintis (1987) argue that education serves to maintain the existing capitalist exploitative socio economic order. It brings in an ideology of compliance with the status quo. In the process education creates a docile and adaptive labour force which serves the interests of the power structure in the economy. In the long run all this would be detrimental to the stability and continued growth of the economy. Inequality, poverty and discontent would lead to conflict. The conflict theorists concede that education helps promote productivity, skills and knowledge, but for whose advantage.

The modernisation theories steer the middle road to development and the role of education. They argue that there is a direct relationship between development, socio economic growth and education. Education is seen as a vehicle for conveying change in the individual which promotes greater productivity, work efficiency, and awareness of events elsewhere. So education has modernising influences on knowledge, skills, norms, values and behaviour. McLelland in Fagerlind and Saha (1983) says that for a society to become modern, it must be composed of a modern population which understands social, economic, technological and political dynamics. McLelland explains why certain societies are more advanced than others. Some societies have attained higher levels of socio economic and technological organisation through an education that allows for work culture, individual enterprise, motivation, and modal personalities. The modernisation theory contends that education in general, and schooling in particular, is the most important agent for transforming a traditional society into a modern one.

The theories of development grapple with what humanity has been struggling with through out the ages. Improvement of the human mind, intellect and personality is the key to human progress, economic, social growth and development. Cognitive, psychomotor, creative and affective domains of humans are vital to survival and advancement of society. This is the province, and operating theatre, of schooling and education.

The invention of literacy, first by the Nubians in Egypt, was fundamental for modernisation, production and communication to occur (Mutubuki 2003). The magic of writing, alphabet, numerals, paper, pen and ink revolutionised communication of knowledge, skills, ideas and events. With writing, it became possible for events and processes to be recorded accurately and permanently. Knowledge, skills, ideas and activities were widely and quickly disseminated within, and across, generations and lands. Trade, commerce, economics, politics, religion, and human interaction were transformed. Writing, reading, calculating greatly reduced the margin of error, and misrepresentation. These skills made it possible for individuals and groups, to validate knowledge for themselves, rather than depend on credibility, interpretation and inaccuracy of accounts of others.

Education represents a major agent for change and development. Nevertheless, massive investment in education can be detrimental to socio economic growth. Basic education is essential but not secondary and tertiary education. Massive expenditure in secondary and tertiary education diverts the funds needed for industrial and commercial investment. Without employment opportunities in commerce and industry, the secondary and tertiary graduates would be unemployed leading to poverty.

Education can contribute immensely to development through appropriate, relevant curricula, content, pedagogy and didactics. The Phelps-Stokes Report (1925) recommended that education in colonial Zimbabwe be adapted to the mentality, aptitudes, occupations and traditions of the various peoples, conserving as far as possible all sound and healthy elements in the fabric of their socio economic life. Calls for relevant education theory and practice continue to be made. UNICEF (2004) emphasised that every child has a right to a system of education that values the child's socio culture, knowledge, language and community. Shizha (2005) underlines the need to include indigenous environmental knowledge in school curricula. Prominence should be given to local and indigenous knowledge systems as a basis for learning and teaching, especially in basic education. Universal knowledge systems should be part and parcel of local knowledge. They should complement each other. Jegede (2000) strongly advocates that there should be a serious revamp of the school curriculum such that it incorporates local knowledge especially in science, mathematics, geography, and socio economics.

An analysis of the Zimbabwean education system helps to illustrate Africa's development problems. For the past 14 years, that is 1998 to 2013, more than 3 million pupils sat for the ordinary level examinations only 470 000 passed with 5 or more subjects (Zimbabwe Schools Examinations Council, 2012). In other words over 2 500 000 pupils failed their ordinary level examinations. The critical question to ask is what happened to them? The system is akin to a train that disposes of its human cargo at high speed without stopping.

Causes for the failure and attrition rates are linked to socio economic growth and development. Shizha (2013) alluded to a number of causal factors. The education system is under funded especially the learning and teaching operations. Ninety three per cent of the education budget goes to salaries leaving only 7% for other activities. Poor governance and socio economic policies such as land resource allocation, selective social services have led to problematic social, political and educational environments. All these have resulted in low teaching staff morale. The highest percentage of emigrants, to other countries, constitutes teaching staff. As a result training and teaching standards have fallen due to lack of expertise, brain drain and poor remuneration. Irrelevant curricula concentrating on academic matters, instead of relevant practical skills proliferate. The mushrooming of schools has led to poor administration, lack of funding and poor infrastructure.

Critics also complain of the Zimbabwe Schools Examinations Council's own economic and management problems. Because of poor funding it cannot monitor the examination process in the myriad of school examination centres countrywide. Reports of corruption and irregularities involving teachers, heads and administrators mar the examination process and results.

Summation

The role of education in development takes critical centre stage. Socio economic, political and other factors are pivotal to education and development. Together they chart the path and course of sustained development.

Sustainable development does not only mean industrial and commercial productivity. It includes appreciation, and conservation of natural resources such as fauna, flora, water sources, soil and the atmosphere by the people. Local knowledge systems play a pivotal role in conservation education.

Learning and Teaching Structures for Outdoor World – an Environment Friendly Model to Ecotourism

People, young and old, in developing and developed countries face many challenges in life. These range from poverty, unemployment, over-crowding, idleness, pollution and environmental degradation. As people grow up and old they need to learn how to cope with the myriad of challenges in life. With the ever increasing pressure on resources educationists, planners and developers are looking for alternatives to traditional models of urban centred learning. So the outdoor world offers unlimited sources and opportunities for learning and teaching experiences. The farm, hill, river, forest, weir, nature trail, camp site provide ample opportunities to appreciate, manipulate, interact and explore nature in the natural setting.

Learning through the use of the surrounding environment makes learning experiences real, relevant, permanent and sustainable. Peters (1996) lauds these linkages in learning and teaching that lead to physical and mental explorations of the environment. These make us appreciate colour, shape, form, structure, characteristics and behaviour of fauna and flora, the beauty of nature. All this leads us to know the symbiotic nature, and our place in the eco system as well as the scheme of things. Hence, studies in eco tourism facilitate the acquisition of nature's knowledge base. And the best place to acquire all the essential natural knowledge is the physical, social and natural environment itself.

Non degraded eco systems such as the country side, forests, arid regions, swamps and water reserves offer exceptional knowledge, skills, and bases about the maintenance of diverse eco systems, human survival, prerequisites of animal and human life on planet earth. These prerequisites involve natural disaster risk reduction strategies that protect life and environment on earth. This includes fauna and flora that are crucial to preventive and curative medicines, and the general protection mechanisms involving local and regional environments. Ogens (1991).

Other factors necessitating the learning of the outdoor natural world reside in the tourism industry. Higher levels of consumer wealth in the booming economies of developed and developing countries have seen an increasing desire of city and urban dwellers to experience the natural out-door world and its complex, yet simple life. Improved tourism infrastructure and access to media, internet and satellite imaging have made the world a much smaller, and more accessible place for people to explore. Eco tourism is growing strong as people look to escape burgeoning urban populations, pressures and problems. So urban and city people want to escape the rat race.

The other factor is that eco tourism offers opportunities for employment since businesses can be started as green field ventures, hobbies or pet projects. These can eventually grow into successful, independent and profitable enterprises. Moreover, not much land and capital are needed to start the venture...given open, virgin small holdings that can combine to form ventures in East, Central and Southern Africa. Well protected and managed eco tourism resources are infinite. The sustainable nature of unexploited natural resources can lead to sustainable economic growth and development from generation to generation.

Starting an Eco tourism Venture

Learners in environmental studies, and science can start, as individuals or groups, eco tourism ventures on an experimental basis. These can later grow into viable business projects. These ventures could focus on giving visitors the opportunity to experience environmentally based products or activities. Examples are nature trail, bird and animal watching, donkey rides, attractive scenery watching the sun rise and fall over a panoramic out crop. Other activities could be nature vacations, hiking, fishing, anti-poaching patrols, camping, herding cattle, sheep and goats. Bio botanical trails can offer learners invaluable diverse learning experiences. Advanced courses for those interested in developing eco tourism ventures could be run by specialists in the natural local environment. These tourism courses would include skills in people management; organising, planning logistics; catering and hospitality; construction and building of tourism structures.

Before starting an eco tourist venture building and construction designs and structures are an integral part of eco tourism ventures. The designs and structures should be innovative, of local content, inexpensive, attractive, beautiful, refreshing and different.

Developing Eco tourism Ventures

The success of eco tourism ventures is directly linked to the amount and quality of research and product development done beforehand. Planning is crucial in terms of market, target groups, information and the product itself. The product needs developing. The goal is to develop a product that visitors find worthwhile spending their time, effort and money on. Basic infrastructure must be in place such as water, shelter, power, sanitation and access to roads. Though the levels of service offered to visitors improve with time and experience, the aim should be to reach a certain standard and product professionalism. Hence, choice and training of staff are essential. Dedicated, interested, hardworking, tolerant, cheerful, enthusiastic, attentive and friendly staff, make eco tourism memorable and worthwhile.

Product Research

There is also the need to analyse availability of other resources such as finance, skills, expertise, experience and support networks. Product research involves service types, visiting similar existing operations, gathering relevant information, compiling budgets, building designs and structures, and other planning tools. The chosen product can then be developed based on the identified target market such as business or corporate sectors, vacationing families, casual travellers, wedding parties, or visiting students. The building structures should be designed and constructed on the basis of available resources to blend with the environment, and to cut costs.

Marketing the Eco tourism Venture

The next crucial step, after setting up the eco-tourism venture, is to market and promote the chosen products using different media like the internet, print media, local tourism bureaus, travel publications and festivals. Public relations through personal contacts, building and maintaining relations with the media can pay ample dividends. A well designed, attractive but inexpensive flier placed at strategic places can be very useful. Networking with other people in tourism near one's own venture is crucial in offering the visitors a wider selection of experiences. Reputable tourism agencies who specialise in marketing tourism operations can act as central marketing, booking and payment centres for an eco tourism business venture. Networking and marketing are often more important than just opening a venture and creating a product.

The intention of eco tourism is to develop in people the need to appreciate, value, protect and conserve nature as a symbiotic enterprise that benefits everything, and everyone, in the cycle of the eco system. All this places humans at the centre of environmental conservation that should lead to sustainable socio economic growth and development. Indeed human irresponsible and short sighted activities lead to catastrophic effects on local, regional and global environmental degradation. So an education system should be designed and developed with all these critical aims at the heart and mind of everyone.

Education for creating sustainable futures for all

The UNESCO Global Education Monitoring Report (2016), supported by over 160 countries, endeavours to ensure that inclusive, equitable, quality education and lifelong learning for all are achieved by 2030. The goals of the target aim to lift people out of ignorance, poverty, illiteracy, health hazards, violence, crime and environmental degradation. So UNESCO is entrusted with the leadership, coordination, monitoring and reporting on all countries' performances in the targeted areas. There should be the will, policies, finances, motivation and resources to achieve education for sustainable future for all. At present the world statistics on school attendance, even at primary level, are still below 60% in developing countries. Adult literacy and numeracy rates are below 50%. Female rates are worse.

Skills for work and life are essential in employment, job creation, learning and recreation. Basic cognitive skills needed by individuals are literacy, numeracy and digital literacy especially information technology and communication. At higher levels of learning, cognitive skills like science knowledge, mathematics, logic, aesthetics have to be learnt. Non cognitive skills of creativity, critical thinking, problem solving, morality and collaboration are essential for sustainable futures for people and planet earth.

The planet earth is facing critical challenges such as environmental degradation, pollution, wars, refugees, hunger, poverty, crime, drugs and violence. Human behaviour contributes a lot to the world problems. None but ourselves, humans, should work hard to change our harmful actions and activities. So education at primary, secondary and tertiary levels should play vital roles. In other words, learning is essential to overcome planet earth challenges. Contemporary and traditional approaches involving schools and communities need innovation, reshaping and refocusing. Lifelong learning should be done through work and daily life. Formal and informal education, government agencies, social groups, labour organizations, and private sector can all help change individual and collective human behaviour.

The world economies need transformation. There should be prosperity for all through sustainable inclusive production and consumption of resources. Education of good quality can contribute a lot to sound economies where everyone has access to good food, accommodation, health, sanitation and leisure. Lifelong learning of skills, knowledge and attitudes can contribute to long term socio economic growth.

People, local, regional and international, need inclusive and equal social development. Social development is compatible with democracy, justice and human rights. People need to learn social etiquette, basic human rights, fairness and equality. We all belong to the world, the global village. People should not believe, or be persuaded by, demagogues, racists, tribalists, fanatics and bigoted nationalists. Peace, access to justice and political participation need to be learnt in school, out of school and in life.

For Review

Education in Africa is irrelevant to environmental, social, cultural, economic and ideological development. Discuss. Suggest an eco tourism venture appropriate to your area. Suggest, and justify three innovative approaches to lifelong learning of sustainable futures for all.

Alternative Development Strategies

This chapter assumes that the reader has been exposed to many alternatives to development and education through the theories and view points of leading socio economists, development specialists and educationists. Together we have explored, perused, observed and criticised them in an effort to develop own perspectives on development challenges. Possible solutions were proffered giving rise to debatable issues. No single solution suffices in bringing development goals.

This chapter endeavours to look at alternative development strategies regarding education in particular. There are serious concerns regarding the efficacy, and effectiveness, of education in meeting the demands of employment, the work place and socio economic growth and development. Critics argue that there is a breakdown between schools and what happens in the school of life. If what people get from schools was all they needed to survive, the human species would have long been extinct. Obsolete, irrelevant and erroneous knowledge, skills and attitudes are passed on to learners as bona fide facts existing in the real world of living, working and surviving. Schools can be viewed as museums of virtue, out of date knowledge and skills.

In the process school systems produce knowledge and skill misfits. In the worst scenario the school products are unemployable. It is like trying to put round pegs into square holes. Schools also tend to over produce secondary and tertiary students regardless of relevance of content, knowledge and skills. The mismatch, and over production of certified secondary and tertiary graduates leads to too many people chasing too few jobs. All this leads to qualifications inflation, called the diploma disease. Dore (1986).

The main competing ideologies are capitalism and socialism. Capitalism dominates the socio economy, polity and education. The tenets of capitalism are ownership of private property, means and forces of production. Goods and services are based on the laws of supply and demand. Capitalism fosters competition in life over resources, employment and benefits for personal and individual gratification. In the process classes emerge with different access to resources, income, residential places, employment opportunities and education.

Socialism

Socialism on the other hand rejects individual driven strategies to ownership of resources, means and forces of production such as raw materials, productive land, buildings, infrastructure, factories, technology and markets. These nature-given resources should be available to all. There should be collective access, ownership and consumption of the fruits and products of the economy. There should be no classes given that all people should have equal access to resources, benefits, accommodation, employment and education.

Socialism draws a lot from Marxian and Marxist political economy. Karl Marx observed that in order to survive, humans have to produce food, material things, draw water for domestic and industrial purposes. In doing so, they enter into social relationships with other people. From the simple hunting band to complex commercial and industrial activities, production is a social enterprise. But production also involves the manufacturing, technical and technological aspects Marx called means and forces of production. These include land, raw materials, scientific know how, machinery and markets. Each stage in the development of means and forces of production corresponds with a particular set of social relationships. The means and forces of production, with their sets of social relationships, form the socio economic base, Marx called the infrastructure. The resultant aspects of society such as social classes, group interests develop into political, legal, religious and educational institutions, Marx called the superstructure. The superstructure is determined and shaped by the infrastructure. A major change in the infrastructure would produce a corresponding change in the superstructure. All societies contain basic contradictions such as different desires, interests and perceived needs. Groups as classes emerge leading to conflict as some classes felt exploited and oppressed. With time, energy and social spring, the contradictions would inevitably lead to conflict and change. The inevitable historical social change would be from feudalism, capitalism, socialism and eventually, to communism, where there would be total equality. In short Marxian theory has been interpreted in various forms by Marxists, neo Marxists to form socialism.

So socialists range from those who advocate a classless society, collective ownership of all resources, means and forces of production to those who believe in the 'Robin Hood' idea of taking from the rich to give to the poor. (Hoppe (1998). However, the common characteristics of socialism are centralised economy, collective ownership of resources, selective leadership rather than meritocracy via democratic route. The goals of socialism are to protect resources from exploitation by capitalists, security of state, co-operative effort for the common good.

Socialist education should conscientise the mind, inculcate socialist values, eradicate inequalities, emphasise vocational and technical work through theory and praxis. The ultimate goal of education is to develop self sufficiency and self reliance at personal, group and national levels.

There are limitations inherent in socialism. People work harder, more efficiently and conscientiously at individual tasks than in a group. Humans do not come from heaven, so to speak. They do not inhabit Utopia land. They want, here on earth, personal comfort, pride, things that give them creature comfort. Besides, people come into the world as individuals so it is difficult to expect them to work as one. Moreover, total equality, as espoused by ardent socialists, overlooks the diversity of individual talents, tastes and needs. Selective leadership style leaves out others from the orbit of power. This has tended to create dictators and autocrats. Individual choice, decision and freedom are sub-ordinated to the will of the state and its leadership. Socialism lacks the method to, rationally, and fairly, allocate resources, means and forces of production. Countries that have been socialistic have moved away from collective ownership of resources towards individual and corporate operations. Examples are Angola, China, Cuba, Mozambique, Tanzania and Zimbabwe.

Nevertheless, socialism pricks the conscience of capitalists who think they have the right to world resources, means, forces and fruits of production. All these belong to all the global inhabitants. There is need to share the wealth equitably. A world of varied and wide disparities of income, standards of living cannot be said to be developed. We owe it to everyone that we develop together according to our ability, capacity and socio economic environment. Sustainable development means the world should endeavour to help one another up the ladder of life and well being. It is not much to ask of the richer nations.

Collectivism

Collectivism is a philosophy, a world-view, which draws a lot from socialism.

It is a theory that believes in the pooling of resources under a group. So the group is the fundamental unit of socio economic production, distribution and consumption. Copper (2002) says collectivism refers to the moral, economic, political and social outlook that emphasises the interdependence of every human in some collective grouping . So priority group goals override individual goals. Collectivism holds the view that the whole is greater than the sum of its parts. It places emphasis on group solidarity, value consensus, work ethics and naturalism.

Collectivism can be divided into 'horizontal' and 'vertical' collectivism. In horizontal collectivism equality is stressed and individuals are interwoven with their in-groups. Collective planning, designing and implementation are the hallmarks of the organisation. Horizontal collectivism constitutes voluntary communes where people live and work together on communal socio economic programmes. Examples of these communes are the Israeli Kibbutzim, the Freetown Christiania in Denmark.

Vertical collectivism, sometimes called socio political collectivism, is wherein individuals submit to hierarchical authority, and are willing to sacrifice themselves for the good of the system. The command economy controls all industrial, commercial and agricultural production and distribution. All social institutions like education, communication, technology, ideology are centrally regulated and controlled. Examples of vertical collectivism are the Roman Catholic Church with the Vatican its headquarters under the Pope, Mao Tse Tung's China, Fidel Castro's Cuba, Nyerere's Tanzania and the former Soviet Union.

The process and practice of collectivism is collectivisation. The socio economic processes and products are intended for every one in the group, or nation. Collectivisation as an alternative development strategy can be used to meet the needs and expectations of groups, and nations. The generality of the populace can draw benefits from it provided there is a just, fair, conscientious and moral leadership.

The limitations of collectivism are similar to those of socialism. Suffice to say that vertical collectivism tended to be forced upon unwilling parts of the population. This led to coercion, terror tactics, violation of basic human rights and individual abuse. In many cases police state, one party, autocratic and authoritarian regimes emerged, resulting in human suffering, and collapse of economies.

Vocationism

Vocationism is a philosophy that draws a lot of its ideas and inspiration from scientific socialism. To understand the laws and forces of nature, humans need to make scientific study of the world and its environment. The world is seen as being driven by dialectics, that is, the law of opposites. Though things look the opposite they are complementary. In biology, male and female seem opposite yet they are complementary for the propagation and continuation of the species. In physics, negative and positive charges are opposite yet they are complementary if electrons are to flow. In mathematics, addition and subtraction, multiplication and division look opposite yet they are complementary.

In the social sciences, victory needs defeat to be meaningful. The idea of a hero needs a coward to complete the social equation. In religion, there is need for the unbeliever to preach for deliverance from evil. Almost all Christians want to go to heaven yet no one wants to die. In law, there is need for the law breaker to talk about justice. In education, the learner, the uninitiated, the ignorant call for the services of the teacher, the knowledgeable and skilled specialist. In medicine, for there to be a doctor there must be the unwell, sick patient.

Out of dialectics came dialectical materialism, a world view that says socio economic and historical events are due to the conflict of social forces caused by human material needs and interests to resolve the contradictions that arise from the conflict of needs and interests, a study should be made of the dynamics involved in the control and use of means, forces and fruits of production. This critical theory has informed social practice. People should be empowered to be in control of their resources at individual and group levels. Marshall (1972) uses the concept of bio power to explain this process of making people be in charge of their socio economic environment. Education is seen as a vital vehicle in conveying and delivering bio power, the empowering of individuals in groups.

Vocationalisation is the application of vocationism to the learning situation. The school becomes a school of life whose aims are life long education, socio economic production and acquisition of relevant knowledge and skills. It has to be education for life skills, self empowerment which is meaningful and relevant to the needs of the individuals and group. There should be a marriage of theory and practice. The learner should be able to survive in the socio economic world through self reliance and self sufficiency in terms of needs.

In other words the group needs and interests should be addressed through vocational and technical knowledge, skills, values and attitudes. The learner takes charge in self development through theory, practice, integrative learning, and work related learning. Vocationalisation views education as a vocation, a full time occupation, which can only be obtained through investment in knowledge and skills needed for survival.

Education with Production

Education with production, also known as vocational technical education or poly-technical education, draws principles and inspiration from vocationism and vocationalisation. Education with production is a system of education that prepares learners for life by integrating theory with practice. Mlambo (1995) defines education with production as one form of education and training that combines learning and production work. Zvobgo (1997) says that ideologically, the concept education with production is part of the search for relevant education which seeks to translate all learning experiences into practical life serving outcomes.

To achieve this, learners should acquire knowledge, skills, value and attitudes leading to independency, self sufficient and self reliant. The integration of theory and practice should be done in all, and across, subjects in the school curriculum. In other words education with production is schooling geared for learning, practising, and producing goods and services for self, the school and community. Production should maximise inputs for profit, reduce leakages, or out flows, of capital. Productivity means adding value to primary products, adding value to shelf life of products through quality and availability of products. Production and productivity should lead to increases in streams and flows of income.

Education with production is a system of education that has roots in African social history. The ancient Africans in Egypt, and at Great Zimbabwe, applied scientific, mathematical and design theory into the construction of structures of grandeur. They used theoretical knowledge and applied it into practice. They were self sufficient in accommodation, food, technology and communication by applying theory into practice. All this is the province of vocational technical education. Colonial Zimbabwe's F2 system of education made commendable strides in marrying theory with practice. Independent Zimbabwe instituted education with production schools that for some years yielded good results. They were, unfortunately, allowed to revert to academic schools. Nyerere's Tanzania successfully implemented education for self reliance programmes. Botswana's Brigades are institutions that have pioneered vocational technical education linking it to skills in agriculture, building, carpentry and metal work. All these endeavours in the countries have helped a lot in developing skills for self sufficiency, self reliance, independence and self employment.

Vocational and technical education has been done in tertiary institutions such as vocational centres and technical colleges. In colonial Zimbabwe these were run on racial lines. Whites and Asians attended technical colleges intended to produce artisans and technicians who would have Africans work under their supervision as skilled and semi skilled workers. The Africans were trained in their own segregated vocational centres. The vocational courses included agriculture, home economics, woodwork, building, metal work and motor mechanics. After independence all technical vocational institutions were desegregated, expanded and developed to cater for certificate and diploma courses in traditional subjects, commercial, technical, engineering, food catering and touring fields.

There have been also moves to integrate vocational technical subjects in the formal, regular secondary school system. Besides academic subjects students are made to choose a vocational technical subject for study for four years. They would choose from an array of subjects such as technical graphics, computer science, graphics, design and technology, fashion and fabrics, food and nutrition. These have been met with mixed reactions from teachers, students and parents because problems of qualified staff, resources, equipment, facilities, rooms, crowded time tables and motivation.

All these moves towards vocationalisation of education have not answered the incessant criticism from those who view education as irrelevant to addressing the real issues of socio economic growth and development. The protagonists against education, conceived and practised today, point at the wastage of resources on a product that does not pay any real dividends to the economy. In strict economic terms education does not add value to productivity, the GDP and general wealth of a country. Instead, it can weigh down heavily on government budget expenditure, diverting funds and resources from industrial, agricultural and commercial production. The protagonists see value in basic and primary education only.

Radicalism

This alternative development strategy draws its influence from the Marxist and liberal socialism. Radicalism is also informed by humanism. Humanism is the theory that is preoccupied with concern for human development through human potentialities. The theory recognises the importance of human liberation from all forms of oppression. Institutionalised social systems and structures, in modern society, cause under development and poverty especially in developing countries.

Hence, radicalism is more than a protest movement against oppressive, exploitative and suffocating social institutions such as the economy, religion, politics, ideology and education. The theoretical framework hinges on de-institutionalisation of restrictive, exploitative and repressive state apparatus such as justice system, socio economic structures, ideological bases and educational systems.

The radical perspective is a view that is aimed at a complete change of an existing system. Radicals advocate for an absolute overhaul and refurbishment of a system in particular the education system. The main proponents of this movement are Ivan Illich, E. Reimer, Paulo Freire, John. Holt, M.W. Njobe, L.Goodman, J. Kambarage Nyerere. They have written books that advocate radical changes in both education and society. Titles that come to mind are: De-schooling Society (Illich, 1970), School Is Dead (Reimer, 1971), Pedagogy of the Oppressed (Freire, 1972), The Diploma Disease (Dore, 1976), How Children Fail (Holt, 1972), Education for Liberation (Njobe, 1990), Education for Self Reliance (Nyerere, 1965).

The radical perspective is sometimes viewed as an anti-establishment movement for human liberation. It questions the need for the existing socio-economic order, the institutionalization and regimentation of education.

Among the chief protagonists of de-schooling society is Ivan Illich. He studied philosophy and religion, not education. He worked and practiced as a catholic priest for some time. Illich laments the institutionalization of education that leads inevitably to mental and physical pollution, social polarization and psychological impotence. The school is viewed as the key mechanism in the perpetuation of decadence and rottenness of modern society. The radicals' salient impression is that curricula and pedagogy compartmentalize learning.

They argue that the content of the curriculum is determined by outsiders, with their own agendas, who ignore the learners' interests, socio- culture and socio- economic backgrounds. Schools are seen as repressive institutions which indoctrinate learners, smother creativity and imagination. The education system induces conformity, and stultifies learners into accepting the interests of the powerful. The de-schoolers add that the education system is the root cause of the societal problems since schools are regarded as the creators of mindless, conforming and easily manipulated citizenry. Schools select for each successive level those who have at earlier stage of the game, proved themselves good risks for the established order. So learners are schooled to confuse teaching with learning, grade advancement with education, and a diploma with competence, which should not be the case. Learners and teachers should be released for the world of learning, the real school of life.

Radicals' Solutions

The radicals propose simple yet radical solutions that lie in the abolition of the present socio economic and education systems. They propose that education is about change, so a system oriented by learner needs, flexibility and variety should be put in place. Learners should choose what to learn, when and how to learn. Learners should be left to learn things from their environment incidentally as they interact. Education should be based on learning skills categorised into foundation skills, transferable skills and technical and vocational skills.

Foundation skills include literacy, numeracy and social interaction. These skills are prerequisite for continuing education and training, and for acquiring transferable skills. Transferable skills include the ability to solve problems, communicate ideas and information effectively, be creative and innovative, conscientious, and demonstrate entrepreneurial capabilities. People need these skills to be able to adapt to different world of work environments. These skills are also a prerequisite for technical and vocational training. Technical and vocational skills include industrial, commercial, agricultural, arts, architectural, engineering, construction and entrepreneurial training and development.

These pathways to skills are best transferred through different strategies from the formal education system which has failed to deliver. Alternative systems, policies and strategies should be put in place for effective transfer of skills such as learning webs, technical-vocational skills centres, industrial based training and work related exchange centres.

Ivan Illich advocates skill exchanges in which instructors teach the relevant skills used in daily life to others. These he calls skill centres, not schools. In the same context he proposes learning webs which consist of individuals with similar interests who meet around a problem chosen and defined by their own needs and initiatives. Those who help others to acquire a skill should know how to diagnose learning difficulties and be able to motivate others to learn. The instructor's role becomes that of a consultant, facilitator and auditor. The learner is viewed as an explorer, discoverer and experimenter.

Criticism of the Radical Perspective

While what the radicals say has made people question many of the practices of society, education and schools there seems to be, for the time being, no substitute for schools as we know them. Schools have been around for too long to be wished away so easily. So the call for an abandonment of the school system as advocated by the radicals is unacceptable to many people, and in particular to most parents. Society at large has got too much respect for schools, and may not imagine itself without them. So society would be comfortable with the reform of the education system to remove many of the concerns of the de-schoolers.

Many people feel uncomfortable with making learners choose what, how and when to learn. So to allow the type of freedom being advocated for by the radicals would result in a state of chaos. Moreover, many people would want to come out of an education system with a record of attendance and achievement in form of grades and certification.

The conflict perspective would regard the radicals as naïve in believing that the education system could change society. They view education as one of the many aspects of the superstructure. It is affected, shaped, controlled and changed by the powerful infrastructure. Those who control the means and forces of production would determine the form, structure and content of education. So if there is to be change in the education system the infrastructure must change first.

The above notwithstanding, school output and performance do not inspire confidence. Highlights from the Education for All Global Monitoring Report (2011) paint a gloomy picture in all formal educational segments. Improvements in early childhood care and education have been too slow. In 2010, less than 50% of the world's children, under five years of age, have not benefited from early childhood education. Progress towards universal primary education has stalled. The global number of children out of school has remained at 61 million in 2010. Many young people lack foundation skills. In 123 low income countries, 200 million of 15 to 24 year olds have not even completed primary school. Adult literacy has remained an elusive goal. In 2010, 775 million adults were still illiterate, two thirds of them women. Gender disparities continue to exist. In 2010, 17 countries had fewer than 9 girls for every 10 boys in primary school. In 48 countries that have not reached gender parity in secondary school, girls are still at a disadvantage. The over all global inequality in learning outcomes remains stagnant and disconcerting. As many as 250 million children could not read and write by the time they reach grade 4.

Questions for Review

Discuss the rise and fall of vocationalization programmes in your country. What would you consider to be the most urgent change needed in the school and society? De-schoolers preach pie in the sky. Debate.

Figures and Statistics for Socio Economic Growth and Development

A book on developmental studies and education should have a section on figures and statistics commonly used in socio economic growth and development. The figures and statistics complement business processes and practice. Figures and statistics attempt to gather detailed information about some phenomenon and sum it up in a short version, statistically. Findings should be statistically significant and not a chance occurrence. Figures and statistics belong to measurement and evaluation. It is evaluation expressed in quantitative, numerical, terms.

There are a number of measurement instruments. These range from norm referenced tests, to criterion referenced tests. Norm referenced testing is where scores are compared with the average performance of others. There are at least three forms of comparison groups referred to as norm groups. A project or business can be used as a norm group. A district or cluster of businesses is another form of comparison group. The nation can be used as a norm group. Norm referenced tests work best when measuring general ability in certain areas like history of a business, business operations and general accounting practices. They are also useful when assessing the range of managerial ability of large groups, in an effort to select top candidates, when only a few openings are available.

Criterion referenced testing is when scores are compared to a set performance standard. Criterion referenced tests measure the mastery of specific tasks and objectives. The results of the test should tell the researcher exactly what an individual can do, or cannot do, under certain specified conditions. Examples are driving licence examinations, operations of specialized equipment and aircraft flight tests. So criterion referenced measuring instruments work best when measuring mastery of specific skills. They can also be used to determine if learners have prerequisites to start on new work; or to group individuals for instruction. They are essential for assessing affective and psychomotor outcomes.

Standardized tests are a result of tests given nationwide under uniform conditions, and scored according to uniform procedures. They are based on a large sample, called a norming sample, of people serving as a comparison group for scoring standardized tests. There are a number of measurements on which comparisons, and interpretations, are made.

Frequency distribution is simply a listing of the number of people who obtain each score, or fall into each range of scores on a test, or other measuring device. It is a record showing how many scores fall into set groups. A graph, bar graph, or histogram is used to express the results. Usually a simple line graph is used where one axis, the x or horizontal axis, indicates the possible scores, and the other axis, the y or vertical axis, indicates the number of people who attained each score.

Standardized tests also involve measurements of central tendency and standard deviation. Central tendency is a typical score for a group of scores. Standard deviation is a measure of how widely scores vary from the mean. Measures of central tendency are the mean, median and mode. A mean is an arithmetic average of a group of scores. To calculate the mean one adds the scores and divide the total by the number of scores in the distribution.

The median is the middle score in a group of scores, or in the distribution. This is at the point at which half the scores are larger, and half are smaller. The mode is the most frequently occurring score. It is the score that occurs most often. If the frequency distribution has two modes it is called a bimodal distribution.

Measures of central tendency give a score that is representative of the group of scores but they do not tell anything about how the scores are distributed. So the standard deviation comes in handy. It is a measure of how widely the scores vary from the mean. The larger the standard deviation, the more spread out the scores in the distribution. On the other hand, the smaller the standard deviation, the more the scores are clustered around the mean. Standard deviation needs some algebraic calculations using square roots to find the average. First, the mean of the scores is calculated, written as μ. The mean is subtracted from each of the scores, written as $(X-\mu)$. Each difference is squared by multiplying each difference by itself. This is written as $(X-\mu)^2$ All the squared differences are added, written as $\sum(X-\mu)^2$. This total is divided by the number of scores, written as:

$$\frac{\sum(X-\mu)^2}{N}$$

Then the square root is found using the standard deviation formula for calculating.

Standard deviations are very useful in understanding results, especially if the results are plotted on a normal distribution curve. Normal distribution is the most commonly occurring distribution, in which scores are distributed evenly around the mean. The normal distribution is a bell shaped curve, sometimes referred to as Napoleon's hat. It has certain predictable characteristics. Usually 68% of the scores are clustered within 1 standard deviation below, to

1 standard deviation above, the mean.

The normal distribution curve can be used to translate one type of standard score into another. Standard scores are based on the standard deviation. A common standard score is the Z score. It indicates the number of standard deviations above, or below, a mean. To calculate the Z score of a given raw score, the mean is subtracted from the raw score, and the difference is divided by the standard deviation. The formula is:

$$Z = \frac{X - \mu}{SD}$$

Some people find it cumbersome to use the Z score formula especially the negative numbers, so the T score is used. A T score is a standard score with a mean of 50, and a standard deviation of 10. To eliminate the decimal, the Z score is multiplied by 10. To get rid of the negative number 50 is added. The answer is the equivalent T score. A Z score of -1.3 would translate to 37.

$$\text{As } -1.3 \times 10 = -13$$
$$\text{Therefore } -13 + 50 = 37$$

Figure 3 illustrates one use of a distribution curve in socio economics.

Another widely used standard score is the stanine score. Stanine stands for standard nine. There are only nine possible scores on the stanine scale. They are whole number scores from 1 to 9, each representing a wide range of raw scores. The mean is 5, and the standard deviation is 2. Each stanine score represents a wide range of raw scores. This encourages stake holders to view individual scores in more general terms.

Yet another standard measure is correlation, which deals with how two or more variables are related. A variable is a characteristic of a physical or social situation that can change, or vary from one instance to the other. In other words, correlation is a statistical description of how closely two variables are related. There is the independent variable and the dependent variable. The independent variable is treated, and presumed, to cause some change in the dependent variable. On the other hand, the dependent variable may change as a result of the independent variable, that is, the consequences of the independent variable on the dependent variable. The dependent variable depends on the independent variable.

In correlation research the correlation coefficient are numbers ranging from +1.00 to -1.00 that describe the numerical relationship between variables. In an animal, for example, the place where there are horns, one finds, in another animal, horns of the same shape and size, the correlation coefficient is +1.00, positive correlation. But if one finds in the same place a set of ears the correlation coefficient is -1,00, negative correlation. If, on the other hand, one finds nothing in the same place, then there is 0, that is, no correlation.

The last but very important socio economic measure is the trend. The trend is a crucial statistical technique used to measure the growth, or decline of activity over an extended period of time. Business management is concerned with trends in sales, costs, fashion, consumption, accidents and risks. The trend measures average growth, or decline, of activity for the time period involved. The underlying concept in fitting a trend is that there is a line that best depicts growth or decline. Several methods are used to calculate trend values, including a method for calculating a freehand trend. For calculation of trend see figure 4 below. Keith and Gubbellin (1975) favour the least squares method. It can be proved that a least squares trend line runs precisely through the middle of the plotted data. Calculation of the least squares trend involves the following steps:

-Determine the arithmetic mean of the values in the time series. This is the mid point, or focal point for the trend line.

-Identify each year as +- 1, 2, 3,4 etc from the middle year, x.

-Multiply each x by the corresponding y value, noting positive and negative quantities. This is done to determine the slope of the trend line. Higher values in early years result in a downward trend; higher values in later years result in an upward trend.

-Square and total the x values.

-Divide the sum of xy by the sum of x. This is the average annual rate of growth, or decline.

-Add to, or subtract from, the mean found in step one the average growth or decline, starting with the middle year. For plotting a trend see figure 5 below.

These trend values can be plotted, and compared to actual activity. One use of a trend is to project it and obtain an indication of what can be expected in future periods. Once the trend has been calculated, it is possible to measure any seasonal influences that may occur. This relates to movement of activity that can be expected.

More information on measurement, evaluation and assessment can be found in Woolfolk(2001), Keith and Gubbellin (1975), 45and Arends (1994).

A student of social science should endeavour to use measures and tests with caution. They do not necessarily tell the whole story about people and situations. The aim is to use measures to try to unravel social behaviour, action and processes as accurately as humanly possible. Research is about finding more knowledge surrounding social, economic, natural and environmental phenomena. A good research, like a good experiment, raises more questions than it answers. A good research should try to find solutions to real life problems.

Information Technology and Communication for Social Science Study

Students of social science should not only keep abreast of technological developments, but be ahead, beyond the horizon as it were. It is pertinent to note that information technology and communication has its origins in space travel, military expeditions, espionage techniques and geopolitical interests. It has recently found applications in sciences, commerce, industry and education. Because of it, the world is now connected with the global networks turned into multi million money enterprises. The digital super highway spans the world at lightning speed. When one looks at the digital world map mounted on a screen at Google, one is struck by the light generated by internet searches coming from every corner of the world. World broadband deployment and high speed internet dominate Japan, Europe, America, and some Asian countries. Huge parts of Africa are dark, with strands of internet light shining here and there. This tells a story of poverty and absence of internet connectivity and activity. Wireless spectrum and speed broadband access should connect schools, libraries, homes, hospitals and other social facilities if Africa is to develop. Students of social sciences should take the lead in this academic endeavour. So a basic understanding of information technology and communication is essential.

Internet Source

Internet sources come in two forms, general search engines and meta search engines. General search engines are Ask, Bing, Google, Google Scholar, MSN, Yahoo. Meta search engines are Ithaki, Lxquick, Surfwax, Vivismo, Webcrawler. All these sources offer academic, research, social and knowledge services

Internet Services

Internet services cover a wide area of operations. E-mail is for general communication purposes such as writing and posting letters, document delivery. Staff and student portals are for conferencing, tutoring and sharing knowledge bases. News groups share news, experiences and information.

E-Resources

These are concerned with electronic teaching, learning, publishing and exchange of academic work. There are e-journals, e-books, e-encyclopaedia, e-dictionaries. These resources are invaluable as desk top, home, library, at a flick of a button or mouse. Schools, learning centres now endeavour to utilise e learning and teaching portals in the process of accessing data, information and techniques. In other words interactive learning is becoming part of the learning environment.

Course Management Systems

These are blog, or chat online management systems for designing course outlines, content, tutoring, marking and feedback. They can be used for applying online resources such as uploading and downloading files. They can be used for virtual class applications by integrating audio and video conferencing, and updating teaching/learning materials. They can be used for understanding new techniques such as computer language e.g HTML. They can also be used for data base applications such as data input, sorting records, Microsoft access.

Internet Tools

These are used for presentations, lecture delivery such as Power Point, content specific such as Wiki Space, Moodle; for communicating such as audio/video conferencing, student portals for designing courses, giving work, tests, marking and assessing. These tools can be used for accessing educational, teaching and learning materials. Web tools are useful for sharing knowledge, ideas and skills. The tools are also used for publishing e-journal articles, e-books and so on.

Internet for Social Networking

These social chat circles, or rooms, are used for social purposes, video conferences to share current news, events, pictures and contemporary issues. Examples of these social networks are Bing, Facebook, Skype, Twitter, WhatsApp.

With this world of information technology, coupled with cellular mobile phones and digital satellite, the global village is accessed almost immediately. The frontiers of communication, knowledge, ideas and skills are within reach of the social science student, in particular, and people in general.

ICT Innovations Reshape World Economy

The theory of ICT innovation, explains the phenomenon whereby innovation transforms existing market-sectors by introducing simplicity, convenience, accessibility, and affordability where complication and high cost are the status quo. ICTs change all business fundamentals on a massive scale and speed. The ICT investment is comparatively minimal. Those reluctant to ICT change call the process disruptive innovations. The process of disruptive innovations requires change in operations models involving business validation, core business, core competencies, core assets and core products.

At present the use of the mobile and internet technology has revolutionized the business and social world. Fixed telephony service has been mainly replaced by mobile phones, short message and internet services. The postal services have almost been replaced. Even mobile services are competed by internet protocol applications such as WhatsApp, Skype and Viber.

A customer beware notice is needed here as regards information technology and communication, especially in relation to secrecy, security and confidentiality of data and information. Recent developments have shown that no site is safe and secure from spying on business, banking, health records, examination portals, politics, intelligence, crime, diplomacy, weapons development, or security. Web sites that are favourite targets are London based Africa Confidential, Texas based Stratfor, and its affiliates. The main protagonists of cracking codes and passwords are secrets spilling and whistleblowers, WikiLeaks and Anonymous 2011.

Their main tool of access to cables is a file decryption key (similar to a pass word) to produce an encrypted version of materials stored in cable archives, official and private. WikiLeaks obtains most of its secret information from the servers of Stratfor, a US based global intelligence gathering firm, with about 300 000 subscribers. Stratfor provides confidential intelligence services to large corporations and government agencies such as the US Department of Homeland Security, US Marines, and the US Defence Intelligence Agency. WikiLeaks, the classified document hacking and leaking organization, to strengthen its power base, has partnered with 25 media organizations around the world such as European and American newspapers.

Another secret spilling organization called Anonymous, hacked Stratfor's web of informers, pay off structure, payment laundering techniques and socio psychological methods. This is proof that no system, no matter powerful, is safe from being exposed. The old fashioned courier services, diplomatic bag shuttles, and manual filing methods protect secrets, confidential information, and security items better.

WikiLeaks Cables has revealed highly secretive conversations on sensitive issues by senior government and military officials in the world. .It has been able to spy into cables communication between high placed authorities gossiping about highly secretive information only recently privy to the powerful elite of the world. The website has gained popularity by leaking the United States of America's diplomatic cables containing information sent from US embassies around the world. WikiLeaks also lifted the lid on the extrajudicial killings in Kenya. It also exposed the dumping of highly toxic waste on the coast of Ivory Coast. It has become the world's most read whistleblower raising levels of mistrust and suspicion among senior political, social and economic players of the world.

WikiLeaks website claims that it has more classified documents than the rest of the world press combined. It cannot be ruled out that more whistle blower websites can appear on the scene to challenge the hitherto secret world of the powerful global elite in business, politics, diplomacy and social networks.

A recent development in the information technology area involves national governments and their secret spying agencies. Cyber security is in tatters showing that no one is safe and secure from surveillance and spying. In June 2013, Edward Snowden, a USA citizen spilled the high secretive spying activities of the United States National Security Agency; nick named Never Say Anything. The USA intelligence centre, at Camp Williams, maintains a 24 hour on line tracking of all the internet traffic entering and leaving the USA. Through what it calls Operation Prism, it has back door access to internet traffic and users with the alleged connivance of leading internet service providers. Professional hackers harvest and study internet communications, emails and phones for what they call national security reasons. Other nations of the world also keep surveillance of communications networks, proving that on line privacy is porous and far from being fool proof.

The Place of Science, Technology, Innovation and Culture in Socio-economic Growth and Development

Science, Technology and Innovation have a critical role in informing people's understanding of the mechanics of sustainable development, developing options for inclusive growth. STI facilitates development of new technologies and evidence based practices. Because of STI significance UNDP and UNESCO have spear headed it as an essential part of the Millennium Development Goals (2013). The two United Nations agencies have made STI frameworks a key component of the future global development agenda given their impacts on key issues such as food, water, and energy security, public health, environmental and social sustainability. The power of knowledge, innovation and creativity is critical for the creation of sustainable jobs and robust economies capable of withstanding fluctuations in global markets.

Improved technology and know-how can positively improve all sectors. Examples are: in agriculture, agricultural technology can increase productivity; in health not only do people need to have access to essential medicines but also need enhanced health systems which promote innovation, ensure access to vital medical technologies. Finally, there is need for knowledge to respond to the double challenge of reducing energy while mitigating the exigencies of climate change. There is the need to promote the development, and transfer, adaptation and dissemination of renewable energy, and other environmentally sound technologies.

A snap shot of some recent technologies, discoveries and innovations that have transformed global transport, communication and social life are worth discussing here. First, the discovery of natural gas, called shale gas everywhere where there are fossil fuels, coupled with horizontal drilling and hydraulic fracking are revolutionising vehicular, shipping and power-generating industries. Liquefied natural gas (LNG) is shale gas that is super cooled to minus 259 degrees F. In this state it can be shipped in specialised tankers and containers. It needs no refineries, is environment friendly and relatively safe. It is finding energy applications in industry, domestic heating, electric power generating plants, turbines, and engines. Ships, trucks, vehicles and buses are converting from diesel, coal and petrol to natural gas. Because of its abundance where ever there are fossil fuels, it is the cheapest and cleanest energy source available. A comparison of natural gas's cost per kilowatt hour shows its comparative advantage over other sources of energy.

Fuel	Cost per kilowatt hour to make electricity in US $
Natural gas	0.039 – 0.044
Coal	0.048 – 0.055
Hydro	0.05 – 0.11
Nuclear	0.11 – 0.14
Solar	0.15 – 0.30
Wind	0.04 – 0.06

Stansberry & Associates Investment Research (2013)

The shale oil and gas revolution will, according to the commodities International Agency in Paris, alter trade routes, change energy maps and geo political forces.

The other important technological innovation is the development of High Band Width also known as Broad Band. It utilises the fibre optic cable that can carry images, information and data in quantum terms and at very high speeds. It handles phenomenal volumes of data, imaging and information, and transmit them at very high speed. It has made cyber communication, infiltration and knowledge accessible globally and efficiently.

The third, and equally significant, technological innovation is the development of the silicon carbide called LED. This stands for light emitting diode. It emits cold light that illuminates but does not produce heat which can interfere with equipment. LEDs are wafer electronic back bone of small lasers found in electronic industrial applications from cell phones, top-of-the-line computers, satellite surveillance equipment, robotics, to dash board lights.

The fourth revolutionary technological invention is the solar liquid water power electric generating energy system. It is similar to solar energy generation but does not use solar panels. Solar energy is used to reflect and hit series of mirrors at an angle, heating water in pipes and containers. The heated water turns into steam that is used to turn turbines that generate electricity. The solar system also heats up salted water up to 500 degrees celcius that is stored for use at night so as to continue generating electricity at night. It is the cheapest, environment friendly and safest way of producing heat and electricity to date. Here is the best technology for Africa in particular, and the developing world in general.

For Reflection

Discuss three forms of ICT innovations you consider harmful to social and economic development. Africa remains backward in ICT innovation. Give reasons for this state of affairs. How can this be rectified?

References

Amnesty International, (2002) *A Report on Human Rights Violations in Zimbabwe.* London.

Applerouth, S. Edles, L.D. (2008) *Classical and Sociological Theory.* New York: Pine Forge Press

Ballentine, T and Nitzschke, B (2003) Political economy of conflict in the developing world. *Development and Cooperation,* 7,11, pp. 10-23.

Barnard, A and Burgess, T. (1996) *Sociology Explained.* Cambridge: Cambridge University.

Barnett, T. (1988) *Sociology and Development.* London: Hutchinson.

Ben-Jochannan, Y. (1970) *Africa: Mother of Western Civilization.* New York: Alkebu-Ian Book Associates.

Bernal, M. (1987) *Black Athena: The Afro-Asiatic Roots of Classical Civilization: The Fabrication of Ancient Greece,* vol.1. London: Free Association Books.

Bhattachryya, F. (2005) *Root Causes of Africa's Under-development.* Melbourne: Rmit University.

Biggs, B, (1975) *Wealth, War and Wisdom.* London: Unwin

Bidwell, C.E. (1972) Schooling and Socialisation for Moral Commitment, *Interchange,*3: 1-27.

Boldrin, M. and Levine, D.K. (2001) Growth Cycles and Market Crashes. *Journal of Economic Theory,* 96: 13-39

Bloomberg, G. (2010) China Reaches Turning Point as Inflation Overtakes Labour. *Journal of Economic Theory,* 104.

Casey Research (2012) *Exchange Traded Products for Bullion and Precious Metal Equities.* New York Stock Exchange.

Childe, V.G. (1953) *New Light on the Most Ancient East.* New York: Praeger.

Chinese Academy of Social Sciences (2010) 'The Lewisian Turning Point and its Implications to Labour Protection'. *The Institute of Population and labour Economics.*

Clark, C. (1940) The Conditions of Economic Growth. *Economic Record,* June.

Clinard, M.B. Meier, R.F. (2001) *Sociology of Deviant Behaviour.* Toronto: Harcourt College Publishers

Copper, F. (2002) *Africa Service 1940: The Past of the Present.* Cambridge: McGraw-Hill

Chung, F. Ngara, A.E. (1995) *Socialism, Education and Development: A Challenge to Zimbabwe.* Harare: Zimbabwe Publishing House

David, C.E. (2000) *Illich, Ivan: Corruption of Christianity.* New York: McMillan

Davidson, B. (1974) *Africa in History.* New York: Collier Books

Davidson, B. (1992) *The Blackman's Burden: Africa and the Curse of Nations.* London: Maxmillan

Deutsche Stiftung fur Internationale Entwicklung (DSE) (2001) *Access to Land, Innovative Agrarian Reform for Sustainability and Poverty Reduction. Paris*

Dininio, P. (1999) *Handbook on Fighting Corruption.* New York: Technical Publication Series

Diop, C.A. (1974) *The African Origin of Civilization.* London: Lawrence Hill

Diouf, J. (2004) *World Food Security in the New Millenium.* Paper presented to the Heads of Parliamentary Agricultural Committees of EU Member States. Berlin

Domar, E, ((1946) 'Capital Expansion, Rate of Growth, and Employment', *Econometrica,* vol. 14 (2): 137-47.

Dore, I. (1986) *The Diploma Disease.* London: Penguin

Dubey, A. (2012) Volatile, uncertain, complex, ambiguous world: The brave new arena. Paris: New Penguin

Duboi, W.E.B. (1965) *The World and Africa.* New York: International Hill

Duncan, R. and Weston-Smith, M. (eds) (1977) *The Encyclopaedia of Ignorance.* Oxford: Pergamon Press

Fagerlind, J. Saha, L. (1983) *Education and National Development: A Comparative Perspective.* Oxford: Pergamon Press

Fisher, A. (1939) Production: Primary, Secondary and Tertiary. *Economic Record,* June.

Ford, K.V.P. (2004) Promoting Economic Development. http://www.nvcc.educ/home/nvfordc/econdev/html

Freire, P. (1972) *Pedagogy of the Oppressed.* Oxford: Pergamon press

George, S. Bennett, J. (1987) *Hunger:The Politics of Food.* London: Cambridge Press

George, S. (2001) *The Debt Boomerang.* New York: R.K.P

Goldthorpe, J.E. (1996) *The Sociology of Post Colonial Societies: Economic Disparity, Cultural Diversity and*

Development. Cambridge University Press.

Graphic Design and Website Development, http:// www.designgroup.co.za

Harrod, R.F. (1939) 'An Essay in Dynamic Theory', *The Economic Journal,* vol.49 (193): 14-33.

Hatt, P. (1957) *The Review of Income and Wealth: The Primary, Secondary, Tertiary, Quaternary and Quinary Sectors of the Economy.* New York: Pergamon Press

Herbst, J. (1990) *State Politics in Zimbabwe.* Harare: University of Zimbabwe

Herbst, J. and Mills, G. (2012) *Africa's Third Liberation.* Cape Town: Penguin Books

Holt, J. (1972) *How Children Fail.* London: Penguin

Hopper, H (1998) *A Theory of Socialism and Capitalism.* London: Kluwer Academic Publishers

Hurlock, E.B. (1997) *Child Development.* New York: McGraw-Hill.

International Monetary Fund *Reports (2010)* New Hampshire: Bretton Woods

Illich, I. ('970) *Des-schooling Society.* New York: Unwin

Illich, I. (1973) *Tools for Conviviality.* New York: Unwin

Institute for the Study of Labour (2011) *The Shift to Services: A Review of Literature*

International Fund for Agricultural Development (IFAD) (2003) *Land, Food, Rural Development and the Environment.* London

James, G.G. (1954) *Stolen Legacy.* New York: Philosophic Library

Jegede, O.J. (2000) *Making Science Globally Owned, Accessible and Relevant in a Post Modern World.* New Orleans: Research Association Annual Meeting.

Jubilee 2000: *Campaign : Cancel all Debts Owed by Least Developed Countries.* Paris

Keith, L.A. and Gubellini, C.E. (1980) *Introduction to Business Enterprise.* New York: McGraw-Hill Book Company

Koka, D. (1991) *African History Notes 2.* Nottingham: African Carribean Centre

Kondo, Z. and Kondo, N. (1987) *The Black Students Guide to Positive Action.* Washington D.C. : Nubia Press

Leeson, P.F. and Nixson, F.I. (2004) 'Development Economics in the Department op Economics at the University of Manchester,' *Journal of Economic Studies,* Glasgow, vol. 31Iss.1, p.6.

Levine, B. (1997) *Life Tools for Social Security.* Detroit: Southfield Publishing Co.

Levine, D.K. (2010) Tools of Modern Economics and Social Outcomes. www.dklevine.com

Lewis, W.A. (1954) 'Economic Development with Unlimited Supplies of Labour' *Manchester School of Economics and Social Studies.* Vo. 22, pp. 139-91.

Machel, S.M. (1982) *Obscurantismo and Liberation.* Maputo. Maputo Publications

Malthus, T. R. (1798) *An Essay on the Principle of Population.* Oxford World's Classics

Marshall, D. (1972) *Bio-power, Empowerment and Development.* Sydney: Unwin

Mazrui, A. ('992) *Development in a Multicultural Context: Trends and Tensions in Culture and Development.* Seragelin: Washington. World Bank

McClelland, D.C.. (1989) *Achievement Motivation Needs Theory.* New York: Power Psychology.

Mcloskey, S. McCann, G. (2003) *From Local to Global Key Issues in Development Studies.* London: Pluto

Mlambo, P.J.T/ (1995) *Entrepreneurial Skills, Development through Production Units in Schools: In Search of Curricula in the Esap Era.* Harare: ZIMFEP.

Modiga, J. (1998) Planning, *Projects and Participation: A Reader.* Pretoria: University of South Africa.

Mohamed Salih, M.A. (2003) *African Political Parties: Evolution, Institutionalisation and Governance.* London: MacMillan

Mutasa, N.G. (1994) 'Africans' Contribution to Science'. *Tonota Journal of Education,* vol.2 (1), 71-78

Mutasa, N.G. (1996) Africa's Contribution to Literature, *Tonota Journal of Education,* 4(1(, 23-32

Mutasa, N.G. Mutubuki, E.H. (1995) Africa's Contribution to Christianity. *Tonota Journal of Education,* 3(1), 22-35

Mutubuki, E.H. (2003) 'Africa's Contribution to World Civilization: A Pan Anthropological Analysis' in *Education Research for Sustainable Development.* Gaborone: Light Books

Mutubuki, E.H (2004) Agrarian Reform and Chaos in Zimbabwe. *Oxford Education Conference on development and education.* Oxford

Ngugi Wa Thiongo (1986) *Decolonising the Mind.* Nairobi: OUP

Njobe, M.W. (1990) *Education for Liberation. .* Lagos: Pergamon Press

Nyerere, J.K. (1965) *Education for Self Reliance.* Oxford University Press

Oxford Economic Papers (!998) *The Development of the Service Sector: A New Approach*

Obenga, T. (1992) *Ancient Egypt, and Black Africa.* Londo: Karnak House

Ogens, E. (1991) A Review of Science Education: Past Failures, Future Hopes, *American Biology Teacher,* 53, 4: 199-203

Pappademos, J. (1991) *Blacks in Science, Ancient and Modern.* New Brunsweek: Transaction Books

Peters, J. (1996) *Physical and Mental Explorations of the Environment.* New York: Basic Books

Reimer, E. (1971) *School is Dead.* New York: Penguin

Robinson, P. (1981) *Perspectives on the Sociology of Education.* London: Routledge and Kegan Paul

Rodney, W. (1972) *How Europe Under developed Africa.* London: OUP

Rostow, w. (1960) *Stages of Economic Development.* New York. Macmillan Publishing

Safrica: www.safrica.info

Satour: www.satour.info

Schlesinger, R.G. (1987) *Multilateral Institutions on Development.* Paris: Unwin

Sertima, I.V. (ed) (1982) 'Africa's Stolen Legacy.' *Journal of African Civilization,* vol. 4 (2) , 40-48

Sertima, I.V. (1991) *The Lost Sciences of Africa.* New Brunswick: Transaction Books

Shizha, E. (Ed) (2013) *Restoring the Educational Dream: Rethinking Educational Transformation in Zimbabwe.* Pretoria: Africa Institute of South Africa.

Shizha, E. (2005) *Reclaiming our Memories: The Education Dilemma in Post Colonial African School Curricula.* New York: Palgrave Macmillan

Simenson, J. (2005) *Africa: The Causes of Under-development and the Challenges of Globalisation.* London: Prentice Hall

Stansberry & Associates Resource Reports (2012) *Investment in Precious Metals.* New York

Stansberry & Associates Investment Research (2013) *Global Oil Value Monitor.* New York.

Stightz, J. (2006) *Development and Education: An Introduction.* Sydney: MacGraw-Hill Inc.

Transparency International, Zimbabwe Chapter (2003) *The Political Crisis in Zimbabwe: Basic Human Rights Violations* .Harare

United Nations Center for Trade, Aid and Development (UNCTAD) (2003) *Africa Faces Prospect of Economic Collapse.* Human Development Report. Paris

United Nations Education and Children's Fund (2004) *Annual Report.* Paris

United Nations Development Fund (2006) *Report on Developing Countries Growth and Problems.* Paris: UNDP

United Nations Educational, Scientific and Cultural Organization (2016) *Education for people and planet: Creating sustainable futures for all.* 7, Place dc Fontenoy, 75352 Paris 07 SP, France

Van Rijckeghem, W. (1966) The Stability of the Domar Model. *Econometrica.* Vol. 34 no. 3

Virtual Developing Country *Glossary* http://bizad.ac.uk/virtual/dc/resource/glos_1.html

World Bank Report (2011) on *Lending Guidelines.* New York

World Commission on Environment and Development (WCED) (1987) *Our Common Future. (The Brundtland Report).* Oxford: Oxford University Press

Wongibe, E. (2002) Land Reform and Poverty Eradication in Africa: Towards a New Agricultural Paradigm. *Development and Cooperation.* 10, 4 pp 33-43

World Health Organization (2006) *Report on State of Health in Zimbabwe.* New York

Zvobgo, R.J. (1997) *The State Ideology and Education.* Gweru: Mambo Press.

Glossary

Absolute Poverty: A level of poverty when even the minimum availability of food, water,, clothing, shelter, sanitation cannot be met.

Abstract: Brief summary of a study's key procedures, challenges, findings, results and recommendations.

Academic Socialisation: The ways that learners are taught to be students; acquire the value of learning skills, knowledge and attitudes; and how to play their role in education and training.

Accommodation: The term refers to special teaching, learning and assessment strategies, human supports, and individualised equipment required to enable a learner to learn and demonstrate learning and acquisition of skills. Accommodation can be put into three categories, namely: Instructional accommodation, are adjustments teaching and learning strategies required to enable a learner to learn around, and to progress through the curriculum; environmental accommodation, are charges or supports, in physical environment of the learning arena; assessment accommodation, are adjustments in assessment activities and methods required to enable the learner to demonstrate learning as well as acquisition of skills.

Accomplishment: It is the process and product of accomplishing inheritable goals. It is going beyond self actualisation, to reach self transcending, that is, leaving a legacy for generations to come. Inventions such as writing, the alphabet, pen and paper, the wheel and axel, moments, the use of numbers, and democracy are a legacy to individuals, groups and nations. Real growth and development are based on accomplishments of a permanent nature and scope.

Accountability: The idea that persons, especially those in leadership positions, should be held responsible for their actions, and practices.

Achievement motivation: The desire to take action, and to excel for purposes of reaching, and experiencing success as one feels competent in achieving goals. It is self actualisation, at the individual, family, group and national levels. Whatever is achieved ends with the achiever, it is not inheritable. Examples are certificates, honours, decorations, celebrity and popularity. It is not enough for sustainable growth and development which demands self transcending, accomplishment that leaves a legacy, for generations to come.

Action Research: Research conducted by specialists in areas of operations for the purpose of finding out strengths, shortcomings in a system so as to improve the performance and operations of the organisation.

Add Value: The process of improving the quality of a product so as to make it more attractive, readily consumable, and usable; instead of sending it off as raw material, or unfinished product for someone to process it for higher profit.

Ad hoc Policies: Decisions made in a way that is not planned in advance with proper research and consultation. Policy formulation is done at the spur of the moment for short term benefits. The approach to solving socio economic problems is characterised by myopic fire fighting techniques that tend to worsen the situation, usually leading to social collapse.

Advertising: The process of informing others of the existence, and availability, of a product; and creating a demand for the product.

Affluent Society: A group of people which has an abundance of wealth such as money, accommodation, vehicles, equipment and food.

Aggregate Demand: The total level of demand in the economy. It is the total of all desired expenditure at any time by all groups in the economy. The main groups that spend are consumers, firms, government and investors.

Agricultural Sector: Part of the economy that deals with production activities such as farming, forestry, fishing, wild life.

Amnesty International: It is an organization of ordinary people from across the world standing up for humanity and human rights. Its purpose is to protect individuals where ever justice, fairness, freedom and truth are denied.

Appropriate Technology: Machinery, equipment, tools that are available, cost effective and user friendly to the majority of a country's populace.

Artificial Intelligence: The application of information technology, such as computers, to simulate human thinking, creativity and problem solving. Examples are robotics, satellite imaging, drone technology, sensor and surveillance equipment. Artificial intelligence is increasingly finding application in industry, commerce, space travel, weather forecasting, medicine, education, travel, the military and aviation.

Aptitude Test: This is a test used to determine a person's capacity, or natural ability, for learning especially in new situations.
Arithmetic mean: The average value of a group of numbers, which can be used to measure central tendency.

Asset: It is used to describe an item of property that has value, real or intrinsic.

Attribution Theory: Descriptions of how, and why, individuals' explanations, justifications, and excuses influence their actions, motivation and behaviour.

Balance of payments: A record of the income and expenditure transactions between countries. The balance of payment accounts records of all flows of money in and out of a country. The flows result from sale of exports, called credits, or from purchasing imports, called debits. Flows may arise from other countries investing in a country called inward investment, or from a country's firms investing outside the country, called outward investment. All flows of money are added and grouped according to their type. If the total of outflows is equivalent to the total of inflows, the balance of payments balances.

Balance sheet: It is an accounting statement which sets down all the assets, liabilities, capital or equity of a business, as of a given date.

Bankruptcy: A state of financial ruin as a result of a business, or person, failing to meet outstanding debts. It is usually caused by poor management, inefficiency, hard loans, or sheer incompetence.

Bill of materials: A list of materials and parts to be used in the production of a particular item, good or service.

Bond: A long term, interest bearing promissory note, issued by a firm. It is not a sign of ownership as is the case with a share of stock. Rather, a bond holder is a creditor.

Barter: The direct exchange of goods and services without the use of money. This is usually the practice in subsistence economies.

Being or Basic needs: Sometimes called growth needs. These range from food, water, shelter, mating to higher level needs such as achievement, success, self actualisation, transcending and leaving a legacy.

Bilateral aid: Official development assistance that occurs between donor country and a recipient country, usually a less developed country.

Bio diversity: A variety of life forms such as fauna and flora, people included, that exist within an environment called an eco system. There is a delicate balance of nature which when upset can lead to environmental problems.

Bio-economy strategy: The use of bio-scientific knowledge, research, development and innovation so as to enhance employment creation, food security, good health and sustainable development. The strategy utilises indigenous knowledge systems involving local biodiversity of fauna and flora.

Blended families: A network of parents, children, step children, cousins and nephews merged into families through marriage, and remarriages.

Brain storming: The process and practice of generating ideas without stopping to analyse and evaluate them.

Bond: A certificate issued by a company or government acknowledging that cash or money has been paid to it, and that it will be paid back with interest. The investor will be buying real assets in the company or government, such as capital equipment, land, leases, royalties, infrastructure, oil wells, or mines. Bonds are safe investment vehicles, unlike of stocks and shares. Bond holders have legal claims to their principal since they would have bought company real assets directly. The bankruptcy process will ensure they get their money back, at least as much of it as possible.

Break even point: The exact level of sales, in money units, at which neither profits nor losses are being made. Questions of viability and production sustainability have to be raised since the business would be heading for stagnation.

Budget: A careful plan for conducting a business enterprise over a specified period of time. It has elements such as a purchasing budget, a labour budget, a production budget and a sales budget.

Budget deficit: A situation where expenditure exceeds income. Developing countries have a propensity to over spend on defence, large government departments and bloated civil service, secondary and tertiary education, and social welfare; all leading to excessive budget deficits.

Business: A socio economic enterprise that consists of an individual, or group of persons, who endeavour to produce and distribute goods and services for profit. Business enterprises can be small, medium, big, or large.

Business cycle: This is the period of time from one peak of business activity to the next. Business cycles allow for review, assessment and evaluation of production, distribution, marketing and selling processes.

Capacity: The measure of the volume of output which a system is capable of producing

Capital: Human made resources such as cash, equipment, machinery, factories and buildings. These are assets needed to produce, or operate a business enterprise. Capital is a critical factor of production.

Capital goods: These are assets used to produce goods and services. They are also known as producer goods. Also confer with capital.

Capital flight: The movement of capital and financial assets out of a country in response to unfavourable domestic policies such as excessive taxation regimes, ad hoc wage increases, nationalisation of land and firms.

Capital investment: These are funds needed to establish assets required to do business. An investor has to come up with a business idea, a plan, risk capital and fund a business enterprise.

Capital turnover: The rate at which assets of a business are converted into cash through normal business operations.

Capitalism: A socio economic system characterised by private ownership of property, , the profit motive, inequality, and class society. Capitalists endeavour to own and control the means, forces and fruits of production.

Cartel: A group of producers who act together to fix prices, output, or conditions of sale. An example, are OPEC countries.

Cash dividends: Business profits distributed to stock holders, in the form of cash. Dividends can also be paid out through purchase of stocks and shares in the business enterprise concerned.

Cash flow cycle: It is a series of business transactions involving flows of cash through purchase of raw materials, wages and so on. These expenses would, in turn, be off set by cash in form of sales of goods and services. The cycle repeats itself each time business operates.

Case study: A systematic intensive study of individuals, or groups, events and situations so as to arrive at an understanding of causes, effects and processes.

Cash crops: Crops that are grown, and produced for sale on the market.

Casino economy: This is an economy that is characterised by high risk, reckless and inconsiderate socio economic policies and practices. Those in authority dabble in unethical, self centred and destabilising socio economic practices such as graft, money laundering, excessive perks for themselves, corruption and looting of public property and coffers. They gamble with people's funds in high stakes ventures. These policies and practices lead to decay in morals, lawlessness, winner takes it all attitudes. All these result in socio economic collapse, worthless local currency, suffering of ordinary people, and general poverty.

Charter: The legal document, usually through an act of parliament, granted by a state to a business enterprise, giving it right to conduct business as required. It is also referred to as corporate charter.

Circular flow of income: The flow of income between economic agents in an economy. The chief agents are households and firms, with the circular flow indicating how money moves between them, leakages from the circular flow and injections into it.

Cognitive view of learning: A general approach that views learning as an active empowering process of accessing, acquiring, remembering, and using knowledge and skills by learners. It is advocated, among other views, by those who believe in de-schooling society.

Collective Intelligence: Abilities to work together by brilliant individuals on tasks and problems affecting their social life. These people would form think tanks that would put their minds and hands together to create, formulate, design and implement strategies, models, artefacts, tools, equipment, and machinery for individual and collective application in their lives. The interest groups would enhance the utilization of inherent principles in matter, energy, life and basic machines.

Collectivism: It is a theory that believes in the pooling of resources under a group. So the group is the fundamental unit of socio economic production, distribution and consumption.

Colonisation: The process of a country being taken over by another country. The colonised country becomes a colony whose resources are exploited by the colonial power. The colonial influences such as language, religion, culture, dress, norms, values, food taste and attitudes remain long after the colonisers have left. These colonial remnants and hangovers constitute neo-colonialism.

Command economy: An economic system where the state owns, and allocates, resources through some form of planning process. This usually leads to inefficiency, mismanagement, corruption and wastage.

Communism: A socio economic system where means, forces and fruits of production are owned and controlled by all the people of a country. It is an envisaged classless society where all the people are equal. The concept comes from Karl Marx.

Complementary products: These are products that round out a production line, to make more viable. An example is the side line production of blades and shaving cream to complement razors; or the manufacture of shoe polish to complement the production of shoes and balls.

Conglomerate: A corporate merger of heterogeneous businesses with a monopoly to produce, distribute and sell goods and services, in and outside a country.

Consumer price index: It is a composite indicator of consumer preferences, choices and the price levels in a given time period. It is usually based on a typical basket of basic commodities of a country.

Consumption: Expenditure by households on goods and services which satisfy current wants. It is a key component of aggregate demand.

Convenient goods: These are goods that are purchased often on the basis of cheap prices, ready availability, easy accessibility; and can be consumed without further preparation. The term is also used to describe convenient foods. Convenient goods lead to pollution of the environment, lack of durability, social costs in terms of lack of value for money, poor quality of product.

Copyright: The exclusive right, protected by law, to one's publication, patent, design, invention, or composition.

Correlation: This is the degree to which two or more variables are mutually related. Correlations can be positive, negative or arbitrary. A positive correlation between variables exists where a high rank on one variable is associated with a high rank on the other. A negative correlation is where a high rank on one variable is associated with a low rank on the other. An arbitrary correlation is where the ranks have no relationship at all, in fact, it is zero correlation. Examples of correlation studies are productivity and profit, training and production, benefits and worker retention, pollution and worker health. The correlation coefficient is a formula that is used to calculate the levels of correlation.

Correlation analysis: A statistical technique applied to determine the extent to which a relationship exists between two acts of information.

Cost benefit analysis: A method of assessing investment projects which takes into account social costs and benefits.

Cost value analysis: This is a technique used to measure both the cost and the value to be derived from a particular activity in an effort to determine whether the activity would be worth pursuing.

Cost push inflation: This happens when costs of production rise independently of demand. Rising costs of production such as wages, cost of raw materials, power and water can push up prices of goods and services.

Credit: The giving of goods and services for a promise of future payment, on terms agreed to between lender and borrower.

Cross over analysis: A technique based on cost analysis which indicates at what volumes of activity alternative means of production should be employed.

Cross over points: A term used in cost volume analysis which describes the point at which it is more economical to use one method of operation in preference to another.

Crude birth rate: The number of infants born alive each year per 1000 of the population. It is usually a positive indicator of a country's level of development.

Crude death rate: The number of infants who die each year per 1000 of the population. A high crude death rate is a negative indicator of level of development.

Current assets: Property or funds that can be converted into cash through normal business operations within a short period of time, such as inventory and receivables.

Current liabilities: Obligations that are due, or will become due, in a short period of time, such as trade accounts and debts payable.

Current ratio: A comparison of current assets and current liabilities which shows the capacity to meet current obligations.

Curriculum: All of the experiences that individual learners have in a programme of education which purpose is to achieve broad goals, aims and objectives planned in terms of frame work of theory, research and practice. It systematically describes bench marks of achievement, content, learning and teaching activities, testing and evaluation procedures.

Custom, or job order, production: The production of goods to customer specifications as opposed to predetermined specifications as used in mass production.

Customs union: A group of nations that removes trade tariff barriers between members. They impose external tariffs on non members. Examples are South African common market, Lome Convention tariff regimes, the European Union, the United States of America.

Decentralised organisation: The process of delegating significant amounts of authority to lower levels of management. It is a sign of confidence in the ability of those working under an organisation.

Decision making: The activity, and process, of choosing between two or more alternatives. There is prudent decision making which leads to success; or poor decision making which leads to failure.

Deflation: A period during which there is a decline in the general price level of goods and services.

Death rate: The number of people who die per 1000 of the population in a year. It is also referred to as the annual death rate.

Debt for equity swap: A mechanism, favoured by the IMF, where indebted countries swap shares for local firms for private foreign debt. It is a form of debt repayment plan.

Debt for nature swap: A mechanism where foreign debt is exchanged for domestic debt enabling resources to be released to finance environmental conservation and extension.

Debt servicing: The repayment of interest and principal on external public debt.

Demand: Is a want, need or desire for a product that is backed by an ability to pay. Demand is determined by a number of factors such as income, taste, choice, and the price of complementary and substitute goods or services.

Demand pull inflation: Occurs when aggregate demand exceeds aggregate supply. It is too much money chasing too few goods.

Demerit goods: Products which consumers over value but which experts and specialists regard as harmful to consumers, for example tobacco, alcohol, fatty foods.

Demographic transition: Malthus' theory says that changes in population growth rates over time due to changes in birth and death rates determine economic outcomes.

Depreciation: The loss in value of a piece of property, over a period of time, due to wear and tear, or obsolescence. Vehicles, machinery and equipment depreciate over a period of time and space.

De-schooling society: It is a world view that believes in getting rid of schools, colleges and universities as they are constituted regarding structure, organisation, methodology, assessment and evaluation. Learners and teachers should be released for the world of learning, the real school of life.

Development: The process of improving the quality and quantity of life of all the people in a country.

Development trap: The vicious cycles of poverty that prevents a country and its people from developing. This is usually coupled with difficulties in servicing debts, further sinking into the debt trap.

Dexterity test: A test designed to measure how well a person can use body parts, such as fingers, hands, arms, legs, to manipulate things.

Differential costs: The difference in cost between an existing situation and a proposal. This concept helps to arrive at a prudent decision.

Dialectical materialism: It is a world view that says socio economic and historical events are due to the conflict of social forces caused by human material needs and interests

Diminishing returns: refers to a situation where a firm, or organisation, is trying to expand by using more of its variable factors, but finds that the extra out put gets progressively less and less. Other factors combine to make the enterprise fail.

Distressed debt investing: It is the purchasing of defaulted bonds in collapsing firms, or distressed companies facing bankruptcy. Distressed companies can exit bankruptcy, so bond holders own a stake in a re-organised, highly profitable company.

Diverse and multipurpose tools of life: These are skills, attitudes, knowledge and motivation necessary for individual, group and national success, growth and development. The micro world builds the macro world. Micro refers to the individuals' private life and the macro refers to the community and world at large. So the secrets of success, growth and development relate to both the micro and the macro world described above.

Diversification: An attempt to widen and increase the scope, and range of production operations. It is the act of expanding by adding a variety of products to the business line. Over diversification can lead to production, distribution and management problems.

Dividends: The portion of a business' earnings, usually profit, that is distributed to stock and shareholders.

Dormant (sleeping or secret) partner: A business partner whose identity is not known to outsiders, and who does not participate in the management of the business enterprise. The reasons for being dormant can be ethical, social, cultural or economic.

Draft: A negotiable instrument ordering a specific individual, usually a bank, to pay a specified sum to bearer, or a particular individual, on demand, or on a specified date. A draft is commonly used in the import and export business.

Durable goods: Goods that have a relatively long life span, such as vehicles, furniture, refrigerators, machines and equipment. It is prudent to invest in real estate, durable goods rather than consumables.

Economic growth: Refers to an increase in out put of goods and services. It is normally measured by changes in GDP.

Economic-lot concept: A technique which attempts to select the most economical lot, in terms of cost, based on certain cost factors. The concept generally relates to production or purchasing of goods.

Economic person: A term applied to a person, a consultant, who applies economic reasoning before making a decision. It implies that the individual has the information, knowledge and methodology necessary for sound, prudent decisions.

Economies of scale: Economies of scale occur when companies manage to organise production on a large scale, and more efficiently. Prices of production are likely to fall leading to bulk quantities and cheaper capital.

Education: The term comes from the Latin word educare, which means to nurture, to rear and raise carefully. So, education is the process and practice of learning and teaching skills, knowledge, norms, values and language. The teacher is critical in the process and practice of education; as the ancient Egyptians would say 'the teacher clears, cleans, licks and opens the lion cub's eyes and senses!'

Education with production: It is a system of education that prepares learners for life by integrating theory with practice. It draws its philosophy from vocationism that believes in marrying theory with practice.

Elastic demand: The circumstances in which a change in the price of a product results in a disproportionate change in its demand.

Electronic, or plastic, money: Electronic transactions are made and recorded for payments through computer networks, without money changing hands. Persons do not have to carry cash to pay for goods and services inside and outside countries. What are only needed are a transaction card, and a personal identity number, to use in automatic teller machines, or card swipe points, called point of sale machines. There is no need to queue in a bank or bureau de change for cash.

Entrepreneur: A person who organises, manages, and assumes the risk of a business. The individual is creative, bright, original, innovative and adept at perceiving windows of business opportunities. The person is brave, enterprising and hard working; and is prepared to take calculated risks.

Equity capital: Investments made in a business enterprise by the proprietors, and belong to them.

Exception principle: It is a management principle which states that routine matters should be handled in an established procedure; and only those matters which are out of the ordinary, or exceptional, should be referred to management for disposition.

Exchange control: State policy where the amount of foreign currency available to local firms and individuals is controlled.

Exports Goods, services and capital assets sold outside a country. The sale of exports results in earnings of foreign currency, and credits on the balance of payments account.

External data: Information from sources outside the system or business. It is the opposite of internal data, which is generated and originates from inside the system or business.

Fabrication: The process of converting materials into parts or goods.

Factoring: The practice of selling accounts prior to their due date generally at a discount.

Factors of production: Resources which are necessary for production. They are usually classified into four different groups: Land, that is, all natural resources such as soil, minerals, water and raw materials; Capital includes human made aids to production such as money, machinery and equipment; Human resources that is skilled and knowledgeable; Enterprise, that is, entrepreneurial and creative ability. So the rate of economic growth of a country depends on the quality and quantity of the factors of production available.

False Economy: It is a concept that originates from Karl Marx, explaining the socio economic situations where individuals, groups and nations are disadvantaged by capitalists owning and dominating means, forces and fruits of production. Upper classes and capitalists exploit the masses and get away with world resources leaving the masses poor, debt ridden and under developed. The upper class become super rich, greedy and selfish at the expense of the poor. Meanwhile the masses are left under deception, unaware of the beneficiaries of world resources.

Family Planning: The process in which parents plan and regulate the number of their offspring, and size of their family. They may decide to use natural or artificial contraceptives.

Fertility rate: The number of children born alive per 1000 fertile women per year. This is a good indicator of the country's health care system, and nutrition levels.

Fiduciary: One who is involved in a relationship of confidence or trust with others. Examples are lawyer with client, a doctor with patient, priest with confessionary.

Fixed assets: Property items that have a long life span such as land, buildings, and factories.

Fixed capital: These are long term investment in resources which represent primarily productive land, machinery and equipment necessary for doing business.

Fixed costs: These are costs that remain the same in total even though the level of activity and production may increase or decrease.

Fixed liability: This is a liability tha does not become due in the current period of operation, such as a mortgage. The portion of a fixed liability that falls due in a given year is called a current liability for that year.

Fixed exchange rate: This is a situation where the value of the local currency against other currencies is made to remain exactly the same through a number of regulations controlling monetary and fiscal policies. Command economies rely on the fixed exchange rate. Its weaknesses are that it is artificial, arbitrary and counter productive.

Floating exchange rate: The local currency is made to find its own value against other currencies. Foreign exchange market forces determine the value of the local currency, depending on supply and demand. Its value rises or falls with changes in supply and demand on the market. Vibrant, confident and successful economies run on the floating exchange rate system. It stimulates socio economic growth.

Flow diagram: A diagram of work area showing the sequence of the operations involved in a process, and the location in the area where each operation takes place.

Flow process chart: A list of the operations to be gone through, the time involved for each operation, and the distance travelled; all listed in chrological order.

Foreign aid: It is the international transfer of public and private funds in loans and grants from donor countries to recipient nations. Foreign aid tends to move from rich countries to less developed countries. Aid and financial bail outs are signs of a troubled recipient country. Poor macro socio economic policies and practices are major causes of socio economic melt down. Usually recipient countries do not come out of the debt trap because aid tends to treat symptoms rather than causes.

Foreign direct investment: Financial and capital assets invested by external firms, individuals and trans-national companies. Foreign direct investment injected into an economy stimulates economic growth, revives ailing industries lacking capital, equipment and expertise.

Forward integration: This involves enlarging a business' area of operations to include activity nearer the ultimate consumer, for example a manufacturer of goods opening a retail outlet.

Franchise: This is a privilege granted to an organisation to conduct business, or perform services within a stated area or route.

Free market economy: A socio economic system where resources, income and capital assets are owned by individuals, groups and companies. Markets allocate resources through free price mechanisms. Private enterprise reigns free of state control and interference. The economy allows for individual motivation, enterprise and effort. Entrepreneurs emerge to service the economy.

Freehold land: A land tenure arrangement where productive land is permanently owned and not leased. Owners of the land hold title to the land. Ownership of land resides with individuals, groups or companies. It is held in private hands.

Fringe benefits: These are rewards or benefits received by employees, in addition to their regular pay. Examples are, vacation pension benefits, education assistance, company vehicle, health and accident cover. A business enterprise is able to attract better qualified staff through its competitive fringe benefit scheme, besides regular pay.

GATT: Stands for the General Agreement on Tariffs and Trade set up in 1947 to reduce barriers to free trade. It has not worked well since many countries continue to protect their own home produced products. It seems to be a gut feeling reaction when faced with products from outside the country or region.

General partner: A business partner who is liable for the debts of the business and who shares its profits and responsibility.

General purpose equipment: Equipment which can be used on a variety of jobs; or to produce a variety of products depending on the skill of the operator

Gini coefficient: It is a numerical measure of income inequality ranging from 0 to 1. Figures on the Gini coefficient scale represent degree of inequality. Zero means there is total or absolute equality, 0.5 relative equality, and 1 absolute inequality. The measure is most useful when determining socio economic inequality and poverty levels in a country. It also shows levels of deprivation and human suffering.

Glossary: A list of difficult terms, with explanations. List of technical, or special, words especially those occurring in a particular text, explaining their meanings. The root meaning comes from the word gloss. To gloss is to give an explanation, comment, definition and interpretation of a term or word used in a text or book.

Goodwill: The value and reputation of a business over and above the fair market value of its net assets. A good name of a business is worth more than millions of money.

Grant: It is a form of aid which involves direct transfer of funds or capital assets from an individual, group, company, NGO, or country to another. No repayment on principal sum, or interest, is expected. But there are usually conditions attached to the grant, direct or implied.

Gross domestic product: GDP is a measure of economic activity and national income. It is the total value of all goods and services over a given time period, usually a year, excluding net property income from outside the country. GDP can be measured either as the total income, expenditure, or output. It is the value of goods and services divided by the population. It is a good measure of the quality and quantity of life of people in a country. However, GDP is not always an accurate measure of a country's socio economic situation. So other more accurate indicators are needed.

Gross national product: GNP is a measure of national income and economic activity. It is the total value of all goods and services produced over a period of time, usually a year, including net property income from outside the country.

Hard currency: It refers to a currency that is convertible, stable, durable and dependable such as United States of America dollar, British pound, European Euro, Japanese yen.

Hard loan: Funds given as loan with high commercial interest rates that can change, with no concessions made to the borrower, or debtor. It is not prudent to access such loans since they are very difficult to settle. It is akin to getting into the Shakespearean Shylock's debt grid lock. So, hard loans can lead to the debt trap.

Harrod-Domar Model: It is an economic growth model which maintains that the growth rate of the GDP, the wealth of the nation, depends upon the level of savings, and the capital out put ratio.

Hedging: A method used to spread the risks of incurring of losses due to fluctuating prices of a good by buying and selling in future markets.

HIV Aids: Human immune virus that causes acquired immune deficiency syndrome of diseases. It is a cause of debilitating, and eventually fatal illnesses that are costly to the individual, family and nation. As it affects mostly young, virile and active members of society the socio economic effects are very serious.

Household income: This is the total income earned by all the households in the economy. This is considered as a significant part of of the over all level of national wealth.

Human development index: HDI is a composite index based on real GDP per capita income, life expectancy, educational attainment and literacy. All these measure a people's socio economic development. Developing countries are ranked low on the human development index.

Human poverty index: HPI is a composite index that measures human deprivation in a country; checking on levels and accessibility to basic needs like food, nutrition, water, shelter, literacy, sanitation and energy. It is similar in many aspects to the Gini coefficient. Less developed countries rank very low on human poverty index.

Human suffering index: HIS is a composite index that measures the level, and rates, of suffering in a country. Besides access to basic necessities, it checks on governance issues, rule of law, civic liberties, freedom of choice, freedom of association, press freedom and so on. A scale from 0 to 1 is used to rate levels of suffering with 0 as the worst and 1 as the least suffering. Other descriptive scales are also used to measure levels and rates of human suffering in a country. Developing countries rate very low on the human suffering index.

Human capital: This is the accumulated knowledge, skills, abilities, capabilities and expertise of human resources of a country. Human capital is critical to the socio economic development of a country. Without efficient and effective people productivity suffers, and the country may be forced to depend on expatriates.

Hypothesis: In research, it is a suggested or plausible answer to a problem. It is a prediction or assumption that provides the basis for investigation.

IBRD: The International Bank for Reconstruction and Development is the branch of the World Bank that lends money to countries specifically for development projects.

IMF: The International Monetary Fund is an international multilateral organisation that attempts to monitor the global financial system. It also endeavours to offer assistance to countries that are experiencing balance of payments problems. The IMF main clients are less developed countries. The IMF manages projects funded by the World Bank.

IDA: The International Development Association is a branch of the World Bank that offers concessionary, or soft, loans to less developed countries.

Import substitution: A national policy of a country that attempts to replace imports with locally produced goods. The policy is intended to save foreign currency, and to encourage generation of employment for the locals.

Imports: Goods, services and capital assets bought from outside the country. The purchase of imports needs foreign currency, and is recorded as debits on the balance of payments accounts. A country that relies much on imports shows signs of inherent economic problems.

Income elasticity of demand: This is a measure of the responsiveness of demand to a given change in income. It is important to a producer since it helps to predict how much the demand for a product will grow as the economy grows. It is calculated thus: Income elasticity of demand=% change in in demand / % change in the level of income. If the figure is greater than 1, then the product is income elastic, or income sensitive. This means that demand will grow by more than the level of income. If the figure is less than 1, then the product is income inelastic, or income insensitive. So the demand will grow less than the level of income.

Income and expense statement: A statement of incomes and costs of operation for a period of time. It is also known as the profit and loss statement.

Industrial revolution: The era in history when humanity applied innovative talents to industrial, manufacturing and service environments; and in the process developed many technological advances. The revolution continues unabated today, tomorrow, and in the future.

Industrialisation: The process of expanding the country's capacity to add value to primary products, and produce secondary goods and services.

Inelastic demand: The situation in which change in the price of a good has little, or no, effect on demand.

Infant mortality rate: This is the rate at which infants being born in a country are dying. Infant mortality rates are a measure of how well developed, and efficient the health system of a country is. It is also an indication of the level of nutrition a country enjoys, or suffers.

Inflation: This is the rise in general prices, and the reduction in value of money. It is a sustained increase in the price level. It is the rate at which prices are increasing. Inflation is usually measured by the consumer price index, against a basket of basic consumer goods and services. It is measured either monthly, quarterly, or annually.
Fuels of inflation are macro economics, sharp rises in energy, fuel, wages and social services.

Informal sector: It is a sector that has unstructured, and unregistered businesses. They tend to grow in out of town centres, owned, and operated, by individuals. The larger the sector, the higher the level of economic disintegration a country is suffering. These tend to be small scale enterprises, with rudimentary machinery and equipment.

Information leaks: Information technology and communication, especially in relation to secrecy, security and confidentiality of data and information can be accessed surreptitiously. Recent developments have shown that no site is safe and secure from spying on business, banking, health records, examination portals, politics, intelligence, crime, diplomacy, weapons development, or security. Web sites that are favourite targets are London based Africa Confidential, Texas based Stratfor, and its affiliates. The main protagonists of cracking codes and passwords are secrets spilling and whistleblowers, WikiLeaks and Anonymous 2011.

Information retrieval: The process of finding information and data desired by whoever wants them. This process requires organisation of files or memory systems in such a way that the data, or information, are readily located and accessible when required.

Infrastructure: Physical and structural networks in a country such as roads, bridges, rail, air ports, sea ports, dams, water and sewer reticulation, power grids and power stations, buildings of economic value. A robust, sophisticated and well maintained infrastructure facilitates economic growth and development. A fractious, decaying and unattended infrastructure hinders growth and development. Most developing countries' infrastructure tends to be dilapidated, lacking in repair, maintenance and up grading.

Information system: A system for handling information that is entering or leaving a business, that is generated by or circulating in a business.

Injunction: A restraining, or cease and desist, order issued by the courts to prevent people or organisations from doing certain things. Ignoring an injunction may result in a contempt of court citation.

Intangible assets: These are paper based assets such as stocks, shares, bonds, or goodwill and reputation.

Intelligence test: This is a test designed to measure the relative mental capacity of a person. Though these tests are useful caution should be taken since they are affected by factors such as socio culture, socio economic status, background of the tester and tested person.

Interest test: A socio psychological test designed to measure the degree of interest an individual has in different types of activities.

Investment: It is purchasing capital assets, stocks and shares in a business enterprise that are needed to produce goods and services. It also refers to a person's expenditure of time, effort and risk in an enterprise. The investor is interested in the security of investment, and the rate of returns on investment. Investment is normally split into two parts. One, is called replacement investment where a business enterprise purchases new equipment, machinery and technology that have depreciated, or have become obsolete. Two, is net investment where the investor comes in a new business enterprise to fund construction of buildings, plants, factories and related infrastructure. This involves high risk, commitment of big sums of money, and good will on the part of the investor. Flight of investment can be a result of a country's unfavourable macro socio economic polities, real or imagined. Investors can be foreign or local based.

Inward oriented development: A country's policy that endeavours to achieve economic growth and development by stimulating local industry and import substitution using trade barriers and tariffs. This is counter productive in many ways. Examples are that protectionism leads to laxity in maintaining of standards, production of poor quality goods and services, uncompetitive prices needing state subsidies.

Invoice: An itemised list of goods or services, sent by the seller to the buyer stating the prices, reference numbers, quantity of goods or services, and payment terms.

Job analysis: A detailed breakdown of a job into duties, responsibilities, equipments and tools to be used, physical and mental attributes needed, working conditions, and relation of the job to other jobs in the business.

Job description: The section of job analysis that deals with describing the characteristics of the job, not the individual who will do the job.

Job evaluation: This is the procedure used to determine what each job is worth in relation to other jobs. It also concerns itself with areas of strength, weaknesses needing attention and improvement.

Joint venture: A business enterprise owned and operated by two or more independent companies, groups or people.

Keynes economists: They developed the theory of the multiplier concept which says that any increase in injections of investment into the economy would lead to a proportionally bigger increase in national income. In other words, the multiplier is concerned with how national income changes as a result of a change in an injection. The size of the multiplier would depend on the level of leakages.

Laissez faire: Literally translated it means 'leave it alone as it is'. It is based on the view of non interference with affairs of people or business. It was advocated by Adam Smith in the 19th century.

Land tenure: The system of land ownership a country has. Some countries have free lease hold, while others have a mixture of state hold land, and lease hold land allocation.

Leadership: It is the basic task of management which deals with directing and coordinating human activities such as business, institutions and systems.

Leakages: Income that is not passed on by consumers in the circular flow. Leakages can also refer to funds or products that leave the business system through illegal means such as pilfering by employees. This can cause serious problems for the business if it goes on unchecked.

Leasehold land: This is land that is owned by the state, or land owner. It is then leased to tenants for a fixed period of time with conditions attached. A number of prudent people prefer to buy their own since a lease is worth the paper written on it.

Least developed countries: These are the very poorest of the less developed countries. They number about 40 in the world. They have very high illiteracy rates, very low GDP, health indicators and nutritional levels. They suffer from acute deprivation such as lack of food, safe water, sanitation and power. They have poor human rights, civic liberties and social justice. In governance terms, they are failed states. Life in these countries can be a nightmare for the majority of the people.

Less developed countries: These countries are generally better off than the least developed countries. They are characterised by low GDP and per capita income. LDCs depend heavily on primary industry producing raw materials in agriculture, mining, forestry and hunting. With prudent socio economic policies, good governance and wise leadership LDCs can emerge to developing country status.

Letter of credit: A written promise by a bank to honour drafts drawn upon it, or another bank.

Liability: This refers to what is owed to others. That is, goods, funds or services owed by a business, group or individuals.

Liberalisation: It is the process of opening up markets to the free market forces of supply and demand.

Lien: A right or claim against specific pieces of property.

Life expectancy: The average length of time that people in a country are expected to live. Life expectancy in a least developed country is 30, in a less developed country 34, in a developing country 50, whilst in a developed country it is 75. So life expectancy is linked to the quality of life in a country.

Line of credit: This is a prearranged amount of credit open to a customer at all times.
Loan principal: The sum of money that is lent to a debtor country, less interest charged.

LNG: Liquefied natural gas is shale gas that is super cooled to minus 259 degrees F. In this state it can be shipped in specialised tankers and containers. It needs no refineries, is environment friendly and relatively safe. It is finding energy applications in industry, domestic heating, electric power generating plants, turbines, and engines. Ships, trucks, vehicles and buses are converting from diesel, coal and petrol to natural gas. Because of its abundance where ever there are fossil fuels, and use of new technologies like horizontal drilling and fracturing, it is the cheapest and cleanest energy sources available.

Macro economic stabilisation: State policies to stabilise the economy, inflation, employment, budget surplus, trade surpluses and money supply. A prudent government attempts to attract investment through liberalisation, user friendly tax rates, transparency, maintenance of law and social justice.

Mainz Income Stream Investment
This form of investment has roots in economic history. The Guttenberg Press, which was invented in Mainz, Germany, is considered to have made collecting regular income, as royalty, possible. It allowed book publishers, and authors, to make money after creating a valuable piece of work. It can be a lucrative and sustainable source of income. Many authors, or writers, have made fortunes out of royalties accruing from their publications. Many people have valuable sources of information, experiences, ideas, memories and autobiographies that make interesting reading. If these are put down in writing they may attract a lot of interest from readers.

Management: The direction and coordination of human behaviour towards a goal or objective. This refers to the control of all relevant activities within a business enterprise toward a particular objective.

Manufacturing: The process of changing raw materials into a finished product by chemical, mechanical or kinetic process.

Market failure: Market failure occurs when the price mechanism results in an inefficient, or grossly unfair allocation of resources. Corruption, greed, lack of conscience by those in authority in government, commerce and industry can lead to the collapse of the socio economy.

Market research: A systematic activity concerned with finding out what customers want and how products are perceived on the market.

Mass production: A manufacturing system that uses repetitive operations to produce large quantities of a standard product. It is also known as standardised production.

Mean: It is arithmetic average used in statistics to measure central tendency. It is obtained by totalling a series of values, and dividing by the number of values.

Measures of central tendency: These are , in statistics, mdexes of central location: the mean, median and mode.

Median: It is the value of the middle number in an array of numbers.

Merchandising: The activities that relate to selecting and buying merchandise for resale, marketing it, pricing it, and promoting its sale.

Merger: This is the process of combining two or more business enterprises into one. It would be an attempt to engage in economies of scale.

Merit goods: These are products, such as education, health, vaccinations, which consumers may under value but which authorities believe are good for consumers. Merit goods have external benefits that people would not take into account when making decisions on what, and how much, to consume.

Micro motion analysis: A specialised technique used to study motions involved in doing work. It is concerned with very detailed analysis of work movement, and rates of activity, which are too minute, or fast, to be perceived without using devises such as high speed motion pictures, timc lapse camera.

Mode: In statistics, it is the most frequent value in a group of values.

Monetarists: A group of economists who believe that changes in the money supply are the most effective instrument a state economic policy can use. It is also believed to be the main determinant of the price level.

Monopoly: It is a market environment in which one group has exclusive power over the supply of a given commodity or service.

Morale: It is the emotive reaction of a person, or group to the total working conditions, relationships, attitudes and environment.

Mortgage: It is an interest in land, or building given by the owner to a creditor as security for a debt owed to the creditor.

Mortgage loan: It is a loan advanced to a borrower who secures the loan by giving the lender an interest in the property. It is usually the easier way to acquire real estate.

Motivation research: It is a systematic study of the factors which determine people's behaviour, interest, need and preference for certain things.

MTM: It is short for methods, time, measurement. It is a technique used in setting time standards. MTM involves the classification of basic human motions, and the assignment of time values to each. It is utilised in motion study to determine the best possible sequence of motions for accomplishing a task.

Multinational enterprise: This is an international, or trans-national, enterprise which has productive capacity in several countries. These are also referred to as trans-national companies.

National income: This refers to the total value of all earnings of people and business enterprises in a country.

Natural rate of population growth: The growth in population due to changes in the birth and death rates of a country.

Negative motivation: The procedure and practice of invoking penalties in an effort to make people perform in a specific manner. This is also known as negative reinforcement. It utilises punishment as way of discouraging unwanted behaviour.

Negotiable instrument: A commercial paper which may be transferred from one person to another. It is a form of exchange which can be used as money.

Neo classical theory: The view that markets operate efficiently in a free market economy. The way to increase out put and employment is to raise aggregate supply.
Non durable goods: Goods which have a short life time span such as cooked food, tobacco, clothes. They are also called perishables.

Non Governmental Organisations: NGOs are privately owned not-for-profit organisations involved in providing financial, technical and humanitarian assistance to least, and, less developed countries

Normal curve: It is also known as the normal distribution curve. It is a statistically developed distribution which when plotted gives a bell shaped symmetrical curve that looks like Napoleon's hat. The normal curve has the same number of frequencies and the same range of values on both sides of the arithmetic mean, its centre and highest point.

Not-for-profit enterprise: Usually a convenient way of holding property by an organisation that has no specific owners. Property would be in the hands of trustees. Examples are a trust, private school, charity, hospital.

Normalcy bias: In times of crises people tend to go into serious denial, what socio psychologists call the normalcy bias. The normalcy bias refers to people's natural reactions when facing a crisis; it could be personal, financial or social. In other words, people believe that since something has never happened before, as far as they know, it never will happen. Almost all people believe so. It seems to be just human nature. The tragedy is that it makes people unable to deal with a disaster, once it has occurred. Even before the disaster happens, it is difficult for people to prepare for, and deal with something they have never experienced before. Events move much faster than people can imagine. But people can simply refuse to see the evidence that is right in front of their faces, because it is unlike anything they have experienced before.

Obsurantism: A world view, originating in ancient Greece, whose intentions were to hide the truth, make reality not easily clear or understood by the general populace. The idea was to develop a pliant, obsequious people too willing to obey, serve and respectful of authority despite its social vices and excesses. Theories of divine ordination, royal blood intervention, natural selection were couched in esoteric language to make the ruling class a necessity of everyday life. This world view, among other things, spawned autocracy, dictatorship, hero worshiping of leaders, imperialism and colonialism.

Obscurantismo: A world view that accepts the oppressive nature of obscurantism especially in relation to colonialism, imperialism and neo colonialism. These systems are viewed as instrumental in the physical, mental, environmental, social, linguistic and economic subjugation of colonial and former colonial peoples. All these are perceived to have led to former colonised nations' under development.

Hence, they are regarded as socio cultural obstacles to growth and development. Coupled with these neo colonial remnants is the African's belief in witchcraft and the omni powers of the supernatural world. On a lighter note, it is common to observe that under those suits, jackets, costumes and under wear are charms for luck in social endeavours; to ward off evil intentions and spirits. On an unsavoury note, belief in witchcraft can lead to ritual murder for human parts, usually removed from a victim live. The gruesome human parts are used for success in politics, business, promotion and criminal prosecution. There is brisk business with medicine persons dispensing the charms, herbs, concoctions and paraphernalia. Traditional medicine markets abound in Africa. A typical example is the South African Durban 'muti' market that stretches for a kilometre selling concoctions with human parts, monkey limbs, lion fat, snakes, lizards, endangered fauna and flora species.

For these countries to develop they have to first of all remove all vestiges of neo colonial, witchcraft practices and processes. In this regard education has to take a leading and central role in eradicating obscurantismo. .

Obsolescence: The process of becoming outmoded, which occurs when a new machine, equipment, or method can do the job better.

Official development assistance: ODA is the disbursement of loans and grants at concessionary rates by overseas governments such as the United Kingdom.

Official exchange rate: The rate at which the central bank of a country exchange the local currency for foreign currency.

Oligopoly: A market situation in which few producers control the supply of goods or services. In the process, they control demand from a large number of buyers.

On the job training: It is a method of teaching in which the trainee is placed in the actual working environment under expert supervision.

OPEC: Organisation of Petroleum Exporting Countries.

Open book account: It is a short term credit used in normal purchasing activity.

Open end mortgage: This is a mortgage which allows for adding to the amount of debt beyond the original debt. This usually leads to heavier repayment amounts and extends the time span of the debt. This should be used with extreme caution.

Open loop system: It is a system that generates information but does not analyse it, nor institute corrective action. It is usually used by people who want to keep the status quo.

Operating statement: It is a summary of expenses and revenue during a particular period of time. This should show the profit or loss from operations.

Operations research: A systematic study of the over all implications oof alternative courses of action.

Opportunity cost: The real cost of an action is regarded as the next best alternative foregone. It is the decision to produce, or consume, a product involves giving up another product.

Optimum capacity: This is the amount of out put which allows the minimum cost per unit to be incurred.

Optimum speed: The best speed, not necessarily the fastest, . Best here could be defined in terms of cost factors, wear and tear on equipment, experience of personnel.

Organisation: The process of grouping activities delineating lines of authority and responsibility; and establishing relationships necessary in carrying out the operations of the business efficiently.

Organisation Chart: This is also known as an organo-gram. It is a visual representation of the formal relationships among the departments and office holders in a particular organisation.

Outward oriented development: State policy that attempts to to achieve economic growth by encouraging free trade, the unrestricted movement of labour and capital.

Overhead: A business expense which is not chargeable on a direct basis to a particular product, or portion of work.

Overlapping authority: This is a situation where more than one person has authority over a single circumstance. This tends to be inefficient due to passing the buck.

Parallel economy: The emergence of a private production sector that takes place outside the formal sector. This is usually the result of wrong and skewed macro economic policies that hinder the official economic sector. This system operates its own market, prices and rates of exchange.

Paranoid style: An evoking heated exaggeration, suspiciousness and conspiratorial fantasy. It is the use of paranoid modes of expressions by more or less normal people that make the phenomenon significant. These include the identification of the enemy, accusation of conspiracy and unwillingness to compromise... fear mongering and manipulation. It is political, social and economic extremism. It is one of the main causes of socio political turmoil in the world.

Para professionals: Inadequately prepared persons in positions of authority prone to making poor decisions regarding socio economic policies and practices. Because of poor training these individuals lack sophistication in planning and implementation of local and national programmes. Para professionals can do a lot of harm under the guise of qualifications, expertise and experience. Usually their experiences are a repetition of wrong applications and practices.

Parastatal: a large state controlled enterprise, usually perceived to be of national interest. Examples are national railways, communications networks, grain marketing boards, mineral marketing authorities. Because of government bureaucracy, inefficiency, inertia and mismanagement parastatals tend to be moribund, and a drain on government budget.

Pareto optimal: This is a situation when no one can be made better off without someone else being made worse off. This usually follows a re-organisation of production, or distribution.

Paris Club: A group of rich industrialised countries that are owed substantial amounts of debt by less developed countries. They usually meet to strategise ways of recovering debts.

Partnership: It is a voluntary relationship between two or more individuals as co-owners in a business enterprise for profit.

Patent: The exclusive right to make and sell, legally granted to an inventor, which is good for 20 years but not renewable.

Peak capacity: The total possible amount of production, working at the highest rate of speed, with no regard to efficiency and quality. The emphasis is on output. This has been the Chinese modus operandi of production especially for goods destined for developing countries.

Permissive society: A society which does not repress expression, good and bad. Morality and ethics are not the norm. Persons feel and do as they please.

Personality test: A test that is designed to measure the emotional traits of an individual, with the intention of checking on the person's capacity to get along with others in a given social environment. Persons feel they can do as they please.

Philosophy: The sum total of an individual's ideals, outlook, world view, opinion, and attitudes on particular issues. These help to shape one's personality, views on what is right, wrong, unethical or immoral.

Physical quality of life index: It is a composite indicator of socio economic growth and development of a country. It is composed of indicators like life expectancy, literacy rates, infant mortality rates, and nutritional levels.

Pirating: In human resource management, it refers to stealing employees from another business enterprise, who are perceived to be better performers. This is done by hook or crook, with the aim of getting the desired personnel.

Planning: It is the process of management that deals with developing courses of action, and patterns of directives. Planning involves determining what should be done, by whom, when and how.

Pole of growth: A socio economic growth and development model that views human development in carefully planned stages that lead to self sufficiency. It is an integrated model which emphasises that individuals, groups and nations should have a central point around which growth and development spring from. The foci radiate basic needs, goals, means, inputs, through puts and outputs, as resources permit. From the pole of growth larger segments can be added to add value to the model.

Policy: A general guideline within which management makes plans, strategies, actions and decisions. Policy expresses the business enterprise's aims, objectives, philosophy, feelings and attitudes towards production, work environment, and role in society.

Price band: Usually found in a centralised economy, a range within which a price is able to move. This results from market intervention that sets the minimum and maximum prices.

Price ceiling: This is a maximum limit for a price above which it is prevented from moving. This operates in a centralised economy.

Price elasticity of demand: This measures the responsiveness of demand to a given change in price. It is calculated by taking the % change in demand, and dividing by the % change in price.

Price floor: This is a minimum limit for a price below which it is prevented from moving. Again, this happens in a centralised economy.

Price index: It is a figure which represents the relative change in prices between a base year and a particular point in time. It is a comparison of previous price levels with the current ones.

Primary education: It is the first level of education that provides the basic elements of education such as reading, writing, arithmetic and general knowledge. It is regarded by the United Nations as a basic human right.

Primary data: This is systematic information obtained directly by the user from the original source. Primary data tend to be regarded in academic circles as more authentic than secondary data.

Primary industry: It is that part of the economy concerned with extraction of raw materials in mining, agriculture, forestry and hunting. There are no attempts to add value to the primary products. Earnings from such exports are low, and not competitive enough.

Primary products: These are commodities produced by the extractive industries such as mining, farming, forestry and fishing. These are in raw material form.

Principle: It is a set of laws that form what is considered, in a field of study, fundamental truth verifiable by analysis.

Private property: Exclusive interests and rights possessed by or more individuals in fixed property such as land and buildings.

Privatisation: This is the process of moving business activity from the public sector to the private sector. The method normally used is to float stocks and shares in nationalised business enterprises to return them to private ownership.

Process analysis: It is an attempt to determine the operations necessary to produce a good. It spells out the proper sequence of the operations.

Producer goods: These are items used in the creation of other additional goods, and services. Production involves the creation of value out of raw materials, and producer goods.

Production transfer: The moving of an individual to a new assignment, or a different area within or outside the plant, as decided upon by management.

Productivity: It is the efficiency with which the factors of production are used. It can be calculated by taking total out put, and dividing by the number of factors of production. The higher the figure, the more productive the factors of production are.

Profit and loss statement: This is a listing of revenues and expenses associated with doing business during a specified period of time. This includes the subtraction of expenses from revenues so as to determine whether a profit or loss has occurred.

Profit margin: It is the difference between unit cost and unit selling price.

Profit sharing plan: An incentive programme in which the participants in a business enterprise are awarded a certain portion of the profits. This helps to motivate and increase interest effort and productivity.

Promissory note: A written note promising to pay the bearer a stated sum of money upon demand, or at a specified time, to order.

Proprietorship: It is also known as sole trader or operator. This is the form of business which is owned by a single individual. It is the most common form of business organisation.

Protectionism: The practice of taking steps to protect what is perceived as one's own interests. This is done to protect local commerce and industry from products coming in from outside the country. This tends to be counter productive as it removes competition from outside producers, with quality of goods and services suffering. This leads to complacency, inefficiency, poor quality products and inertia.

Proxy: This is a written authorisation by a stock holder giving another person the right to attend and vote on behalf of the stock holder.

Purchasing power: It is the amount of goods and services that a given amount of money can buy. Hard currencies buy more than local, less developed countries' currencies.

Qualitative research: A systematic study of interpretations, feelings, attitudes and meanings individuals give to social events, situations and circumstances. It is interested in the qualitative context out of which data emerge. The truth is bound to come from how people qualify the day to day lives in routine everyday situations. Individuals qualify their social world through the historical, cultural, scientific, ideological, linguistic and environmental lenses, so to speak. The favoured research methods and techniques are social surveys, interviews, introspective biographical accounts, and opinion-naires.

Quality control: The process of manufacturing which ensures that designated standards are met through out the production cycle. The demand for a product lies on its perceived quality by the purchaser.

Quantitative research: A systematic, scientific study of natural phenomena and the social world. Like the natural world, the social world should be examined using testable hypotheses, empirical based methods and verifiable instruments. It is possible to find out and quantify the cause and effect relationships, phenomena and their existence through careful empirical investigation. The research methods and techniques are designed to collect quantitative data through experimentation, structured interviews, mathematical models, statistics, interaction counts and correlation measures. It is argued that quantitative data can be reliably measured, patterns can be established clearly, cause and effect can easily be discovered. Conclusions and generalisations will be accurate since they are located in an empirical mode of operations.

Quaternary sector: Refers to service sector constituting intellectuals, or information related positions that include education, health care, government, and information technology. The quaternary service sector is an extension of the tertiary sector.

Quietism: It is a form of socio cultural devotion based on a calm and passive acceptance of life, and the abandonment of all desires. Unquestioning life, and acquiescence to authority, can lead to people being taken for a ride. Accountability, efficiency, social justice, freedom and economic development become the casualties. This is in stark contrast with activism, where individuals and groups will agitate for change leading to uprisings, social springs, change and revolutions.

Quinary Sector: A further extension of the quaternary sector that refers to top level executives in any part of the service sector. It includes chief executive officers, high level government officials, education, and health care administrators.

Quotas: These are limits on the amount of a good produced, imported, exported, or offered for sale.

Radicalism: It is more than a protest movement against oppressive, exploitative and suffocating social institutions such as the economy, religion, politics, ideology and education. Radicalism has led to the rise of alternative development strategies such as de-schooling society, social springs and revolutions.

Real income: This refers to the actual purchasing power of a currency. It is the amount of goods and services a currency as of a given time.

Real property: This refers to real estate such as productive land and buildings.
This is considered real, durable wealth.

Reasoned action theory: Reasoned action draws its definitions from the theory of reasoned action. Reasoned action is based on the assumption that human beings are usually quite rational, and make systematic use of the information available to them. Hence, people consider the implications of their actions in given contexts, at given times, before deciding to engage, or not, in a given behaviour. They ask the questions to be involved or not to be. The theory also emphasises that most actions of social relevance are under volitional control.

This theory is conceptually similar to the health belief model that emphasises construct of behavioural intention as a determinant of health behaviour. This theory focuses on the role of personal intention in determining whether behaviour modification will occur. In other words, individuals are their own best doctors. Care givers can only help individuals to deal, and cope, with their ailments, indulgencies, preventable diseases and other social problems. In short, people cannot be developed. They can only develop themselves. If persons ask for fish they should not only be shown how to fish, but how to farm fish.

Recession: Recession is a period of negative socio economic growth at the cliff of the trade cycle. It is defined as consecutive periods, or quarters, of negative economic growth. It leads to human suffering in terms of loss of employment, wages, housing and essential social services.

Reciprocity: This is the process of returning a favour: You scratch my back and I scratch yours. It can be in a form of agreement or arrangement in which two or more individuals, businesses, countries or nations grant the other's favour.

Relative poverty: It is the level of poverty in a country expressed in terms of certain levels of income, cost of living, consumer durables and property. The general populace of a country would have basic needs like food, clothes, shelter, water and sanitation; access to basic health and education. But the differences between individuals in the country would be on the quality and quantity of life. That would constitute relative poverty, that is, poverty in relation to other people in the country.

Repetitive operations: A series of operations performed over and over to produce large quantities of uniform products. This is commonly used in mass production lines.

Revaluation: It is the value of the exchange rate increasing due to market forces. It is the opposite of devaluation.

Risk: This refers to the degree of uncertainty or chance inherent in a situation or socio economic environment. Investment decisions are based on the amount and level of risk involved. As a rule of thumb, investors are sensitive to socio economic potential risks especially those risks perceived to emanate from political, civic and religious authorities. Unscrupulous pronouncements from those in authority can easily scare away foreign and local investors.

Rural urban migration: It is the movement of people from rural areas to urban centres, in search of a better life. This usually results in more problems such as unemployment, poverty, lack of shelter, water and sanitation.

Savings: Savings are that part of disposable income not spent on goods and services. It is income not spent, but put aside for a rainy day, as it were. In an economic sense, savings are a leakage, or withdrawal, from the circular flow.

Secondary data: Systematic information not obtained by the user from its original source, but from previously collected references. The data are open to errors, omissions and interpretation. Interpretation of information is not necessarily fact.

Secondary industry: Secondary industry is that part of the economy concerned with the manufacture of goods. It is the process of adding value to raw materials into finished products. This is a good measure of a country's level of development.

Secured loan: It is a loan secured by pledging certain property as security. If there is a default in payment, the debt can be recovered from the disposal of the pledged property.

Self insurance: This is a method of protecting a business enterprise against risk by setting up contingency funds within the organisation. It is prudent to do so when venturing into uncharted economic ventures.

Self reliance: It is a universal concept that takes into account the necessity to satisfy human basic needs such as nourishing food, safe water, decent shelter, clothes, safety and security. The economy has to address and satisfy those needs for everyone in society. Education is viewed as the main tool in making people self reliant.

Seller's lien: This refers to the seller's right to retain possession of particular goods until they are fully paid for by the buyer.

Service industry: This is an industry that offers a back up service rather than producing goods for sale, for example insurance services, health scheme for workers, funeral service, skills and managerial training.

Shareholder: Is a partial owner of profits made by a firm, as determined by the board of directors from time to time. The shared profits are called dividends. If the company's products enjoy high demand the profits will grow. But the world of business suffers from volatility of supply, demand and fluctuations in prices. When a company under performs profits plummet resulting in share holders losing out.

Short term funds: These are funds borrowed for a period ranging from 30 days to under a year.

Simulation: It is an imitation of business situations to allow for evaluation of alternative courses of action, or direction.

Socialism: It is Karl Marx's transitional stage to Communism when all means, forces and fruits of production are owned by everyone in society. Marx's political economy moves inexorably, in stages, from communalism, feudalism, capitalism, socialism to communism. Capitalism is characterised by conflict over means, forces and fruits of production. Because of the greed factor classes emerge: the ruling class who own the means, forces and fruits of production, the bourgeoisie, the prolitariat (workers) and peasants. The struggle to wrestle the means, forces and fruits of production rests with the prolitariet, beginning with the control of government and state. The state would control the economy as custodians of the people's wealth. This is socialism. Followers of Marx's doctrine, Marxists, have developed variations of socialism, but the basic tenets remain the same.

Social spring: It is a term used to describe a sudden, but sustained, mass agitation for social, political or economic change. This is usually triggered by collective perception of unfairness, exploitation, oppression and injustice by those in authority. Autocracy, corruption, insensitivity to other people's plight and sanctity of life, lead to festering hatred that need just a social trigger to develop into mass protests demanding immediate redress. Social springs eventually lead to social revolutions. Once people realise their power to change the social, political, economic or religious environment agitation for change becomes imperative. Revolutionary wars, anti South African Apartheid demonstrations (Toi Toi), crusades and Arab springs are typical examples of social springs.

Soft loan: This a loan made on concessionary terms of interest and repayment period. It is user friendly and can lead to socio economic growth. It is a complete opposite of a hard loan.

Span of control: This refers to the number of people working under the effective supervision or a senior person in the business enterprise.

Special drawing rights: These are a form of international artificial money created by the IMF that is acceptable in settlement of debts between countries.

Specialisation: This is the process of concentrating in the production of one good or service.

Speculative buying: It is the purchase in the present, of goods and services in the hope of making savings and profits later from resale. .

Standard cost: This term refers to a predetermined cost level, such as a standard cost for material used in a unit of production.

Standard deviation: It is a measure of dispersion of values about a mean, or central value.

Standard of living: A measure of the material level of living which a person's income can command. This depends on GDP, level of prices for basic commodities, food, shelter, level of literacy and access to health, safe water and sanitation.

Standardisation: The process of establishing specific criteria levels for production, for example mass, grade and quality of materials, dimensions.

Staple food: It is the main food consumed by a large percentage of the population of a country. This, among other things, will constitute the staple diet of a country.

Statement of financial condition: It is a summary of assets, liabilities and net worth of a business as at a particular moment of time.

Statistics: The methods involved in collating, collecting, describing and analysing numerical data. Statistics belong to the laws of logic and probability.

Streams of income: These are strategically planned income generating projects designed to augment each other resulting in a constant, sustained flow of cash or money to the originator of the enterprises. This helps to hedge against unforeseen down turns in the economy.

Structural adjustment programme: This is a country socio economic programme of free market, and supply side, reforms that multilateral agencies, such as the IMF and World Bank, lay down as conditions for lending money to countries. It involves the forced restructuring of the economy so as to promote a free economy controlled by market forces in an effort to promote higher growth and to reduce poverty and unemployment.

Subsidy: This is money given to producers to off set costs against market related prices of goods or services. Examples are producer subsidies of fertiliser, seed, power, mining inputs, fishing equipment and boats. Subsidies lead to sick economies as they encourage lousy economic house keeping, waste of resources and misplaced allocation of resources.

Subsistence farming: Here farming input and out put are for consumption of the producer and immediate family, and not for sale. If any surplus is realised, it is sold by barter, for other goods and services. This usually leads to subsistence living where the people are subject to the vagaries of shortages, drought and hunger.

Subsistence income: This is just about the poverty datum line, allowing the person to subsist. It is a level of income just about enough to sustain a person, just the barest minimum. This state of affairs is common in least developing countries.

Succession planning: Careful and systematic planning and preparation by individuals, groups or organizations for the take over of operations by younger, more energetic personnel. The older generation works closely with the would-be successors, showing them the ropes. As the potential successors gain confidence, skills and expertise in running the organisation, the predecessors recede into the background as advisers and consultants. Successful people, groups and organisations have inbuilt succession mechanisms for the smooth continuity of operations. Succession planning is based on the social fact that no one in the world is indispensable. Life must go on after the leader is gone.

Sunk cost: It is a cost that a business enterprise can do nothing about. It concerns a past expenditure, or out lay, which, by itself, should not be used as a basis for making a decision,

Supply: The amount of goods which producers are prepared to sell at a given price. Supply is determined by factors such as costs of production, targets and demand.

Supply curve: A diagrammatical chart indicating the quantity of goods a producer would be willing to offer for sale at various prices.

Sustainable development: Development where consideration is given to the quality of life of future, as well as, current generations. It is growth and development that meets the needs of the present without compromising the ability of future generations to meet their own needs. It is a sustained effort at promoting long term production cycles that are ecologically friendly.

Synthetic process: The process of putting materials, or parts, together to form a new product, such as making cloth from by products of coal, a car from several hybrid materials, natural and artificial.

System: An inter-dependent group of activities which are linked by organisation intended to work efficiently for common goals, aims and objectives.

Tariff: Tariffs are taxes and restrictions imposed on goods imported into the country. They are intended to protect local commerce and industry.

Technology: Scientific study and use of mechanical, physical, electrical, electronic and applied sciences to solving development problems. It is the application of scientific knowledge, principles and laws to life problems.

Tertiary industry: Tertiary industry is concerned with the provision of services. Examples are education, health, insurance, legal affairs, entertainment and catering.

Tied aid: This is bilateral foreign aid that is given on the condition that the recipient country uses the funds to buy goods and services from the donor country.
Trading bloc: This is a regional group of countries co-operating to liberalise trade between them. It involves trade liberalisation, with the removal of barriers, quotas and tariffs.

Time and motion study: An analysis of the various motions involved in an operation, and of the length of time taken by each motion. Its purpose is to establish a standard method of doing an operation, and a standard amount of time for its completion.

Trademark: A device, name, logo, or symbol used by a manufacturer, designer, or seller, to distinguish own goods from others. Trademarks, or logos, are registered, and copyrighted to ensure that others will not use, or abuse them.

Transfer cost: The cost that a department must bear for goods and services supplied by another department.

Trans national corporations: These are bigger that multinationals. They are mega business organisations that pull their massive resources towards dominating areas of operations, markets and distribution networks.

Trend: The growth and decline of an activity over an extended period of time. It is a crucial statistical technique used to measure the growth, or decline of activity over an extended period of time. Business management is concerned with trends in sales, costs, fashion, consumption, accidents and risks. So the trend measures average growth, or decline, of activity for the time period involved. The underlying concept in fitting a trend is that there is a line that best depicts growth or decline.

Trial and error pricing: Selling a product at various prices in a number of areas, and then evaluating the response to each price.

Trickle down: It is the process through which the economic gains from economic growth pass down through out the entire nation, eventually giving rise to development.

Ujamaa: It is a KiSwahili concept meaning living and working together harmoniously, in groups. Nyerere used the concept to develop a brand of African socialism that enshrined the national and universal values of self reliance.

Under-development: The concept refers to the unpalatable conditions of people and country lacking basic needs and facilities. It is a state of having very low levels of socio economic productivity, technological sophistication, political prudence and well being. Manifestations of under-development include debt, poverty, dependency, unemployment, hunger, malnutrition, disease, illiteracy, school drop outs, socio-political instability, migration and crime.

Universality of management functions: The idea that managers, no matter what they manage, or at what level they manage, are concerned for the same basic functions. The basic laws and principles are the same in spite of the size, level and complexity.

Urbanisation: Urbanisation is an economic process involved in the growth of towns and cities.

Uruguay round: The final round of trade negotiations of the General Agreement on Tariffs and Trade.

Usufruct: A system of land tenure where land is communally owned, and people have free access to use it. This is common in many African countries in the rural areas.

Value: The relative worth, utility, or importance of a thing, such as a product, an idea or a process.

Value added: The difference between the final value of final goods minus the cost of buying raw materials, and intermediate goods.

Value added tax: Tax on goods at the point of sale. VAT is tax on the rise in value of a product at each stage of manufacture. The consumer bears the cost. It is similar to sales tax

Variable costs: Costs which vary directly with the volume of activity, such as production.

Vested rights: Rights which are inherent in a situation, or event which cannot be taken away, such as the right of a stock holder to vote.

Vestibule schools: Training areas which simulate the actual working environment. These types of schools are advocated for by those who believe in de-schooling society.

VUCA: The term refers to the volatile, uncertain, complex and ambiguous world. The ability to focus on causes and effects of the volatile, uncertain, complex and ambiguous world is a skill needed for success in life. One needs to make sense of the VUCA world. A good achiever should have the ability to create a long term vision and deep expertise in some specific domain. This involves the ability to move through the overload of information which clutters the present day brave VUCA world. One should be able to identify focus areas and then get deep into the flow of transformational innovation.

Vocationalisation: It views education as a vocation, a full time occupation, which can only be obtained through investment in knowledge and skills needed for survival.

WTO: It is the World Trade Organisation that oversees and monitors world trade. It is a rich source of development data and activities.

Wage differentials: Variations in wages for the same type of work in different industries, geographic areas and so on.

Wholesale price index: A composite index representing the average price level of selected items at the wholesale level. It is used to indicate price movements. .

Working capital: Assets or funds that will be converted into cash for use in a business enterprise.

Work persons' compensation fund: Insurance required by law, and financed by employers, which provides for payment to employees, or their immediate families, for injuries, illness or death suffered in connection with their work.

World Bank: The World Bank is a multilateral institution established in 1945 following the Bretton Woods conference of 1944. Its headquarters, like the sister institution the IMF, are in Bretton Woods, New Hampshire, USA. The bank encourages capital investment for reconstruction and development in member countries. The projects are managed by the IMF.

Xenophobia: Intense dislike or fear of foreigners or strangers. This is as a result of misplaced perceptions of the socio culture, language and deportment of people different from the locals. Xenophobia can lead to hatred, attacks and social conflict that can result in retarded socio economic growth and development. Education has to work hard to remove xenophobic inclinations inherent in many people.

Zero tolerance: An attitude, a frame of mind, that totally rejects any form of social injustice such as racial discrimination, xenophobia, socio cultural intolerance, religious hatred, and socio economic inequality. Zero tolerance is subscribed to at the individual, group, business, national, and international levels. Regional groupings, the United Nations, Human Rights groups, the International Court of Justice preoccupy themselves with zero tolerance endeavours.

Note: For more glossary terms and details refer to sources such as Keith, L.A. and Gubellini, C.E., United Nations Statutes and Agencies, Virtual Development Country Publications, Woolfolk A.E.